Emma L Williams

Butterfly Garden

Colouring book for adults

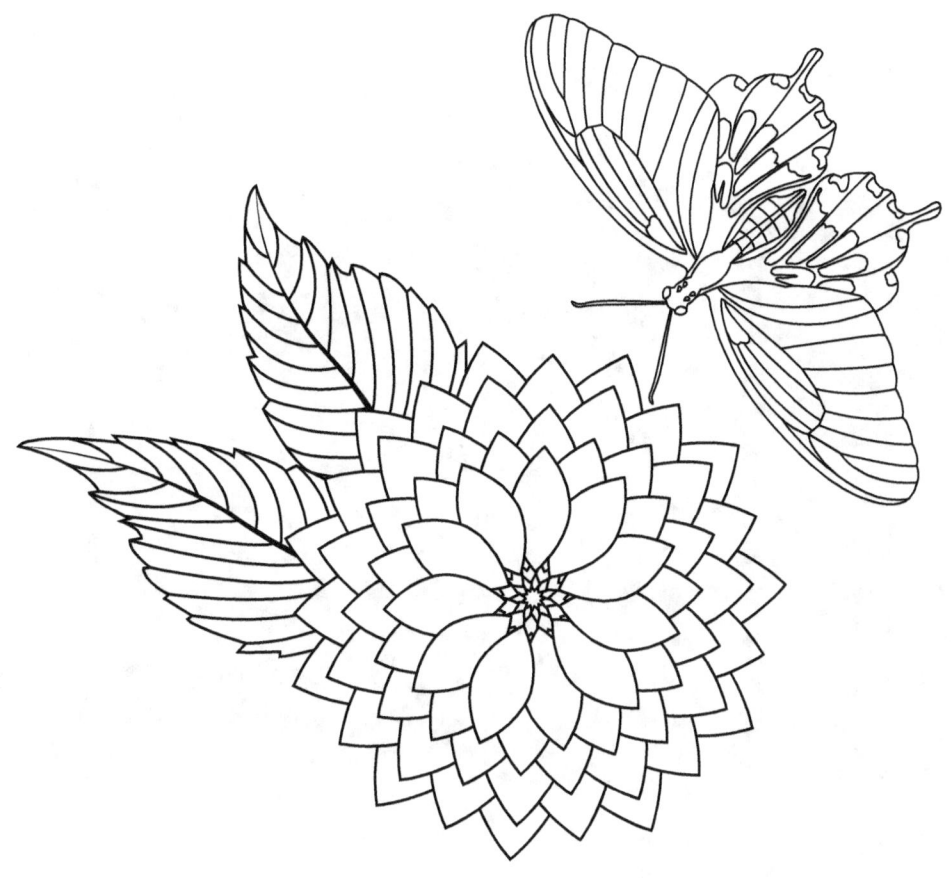

Help yourself relax by colouring your way through these 30 designs.
After you have completed them you will have lovely works of art for
you to admire and possibly hang on your walls.

I hope you enjoy these pages as much as i did creating them and to add a
little bit of fun why not try to name what species of butterfly they are and
flora within the designs

(answers in the back of the book).

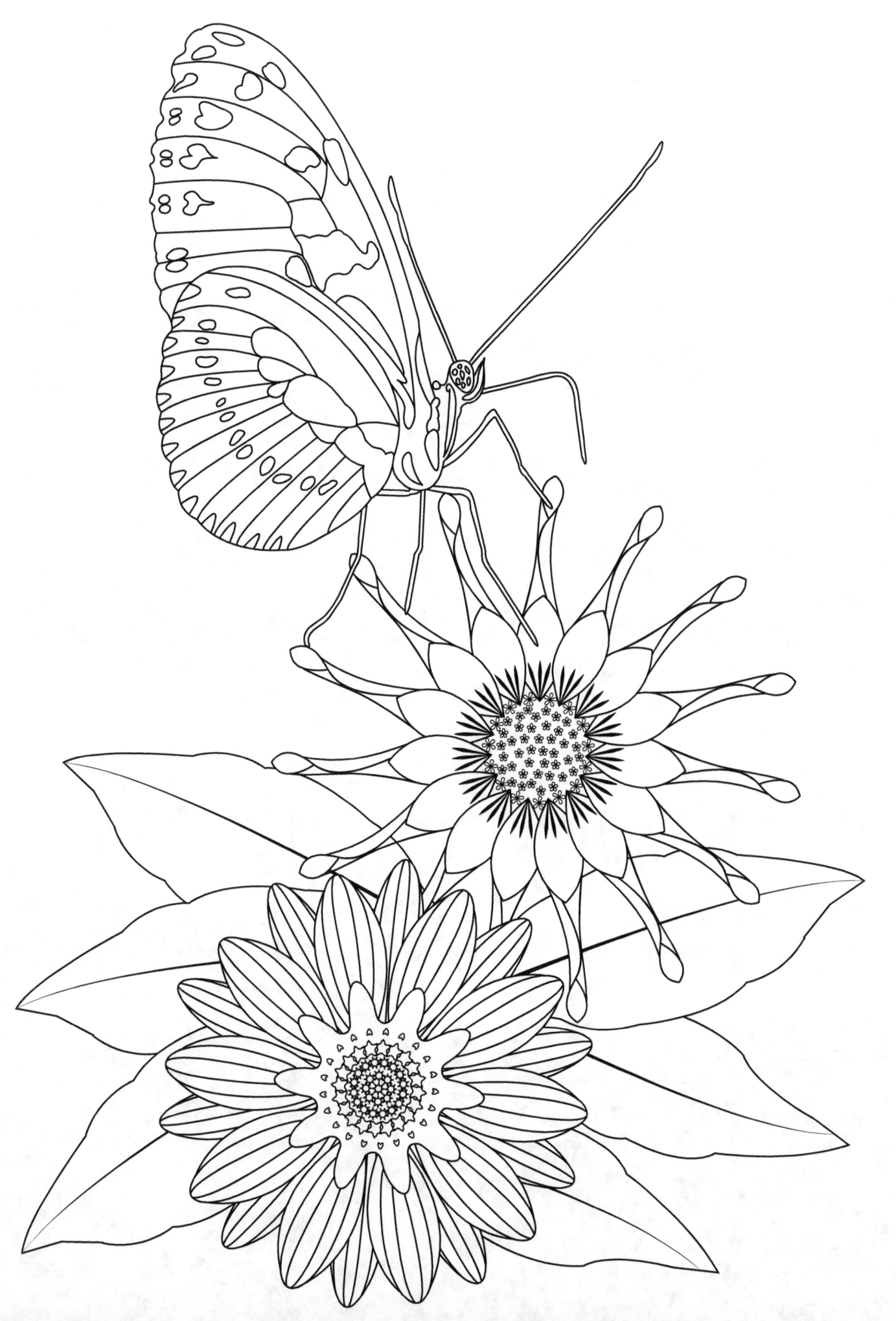

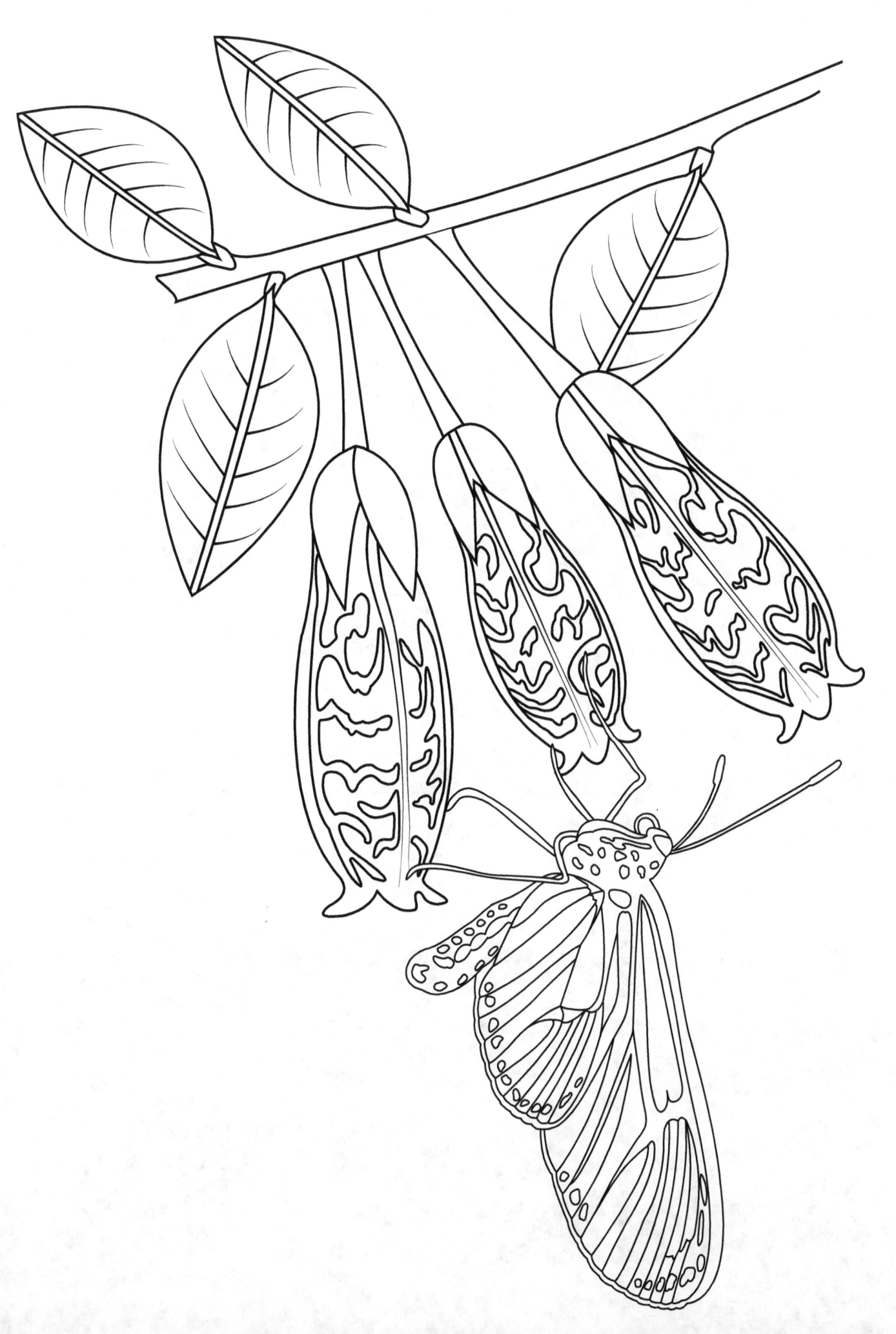

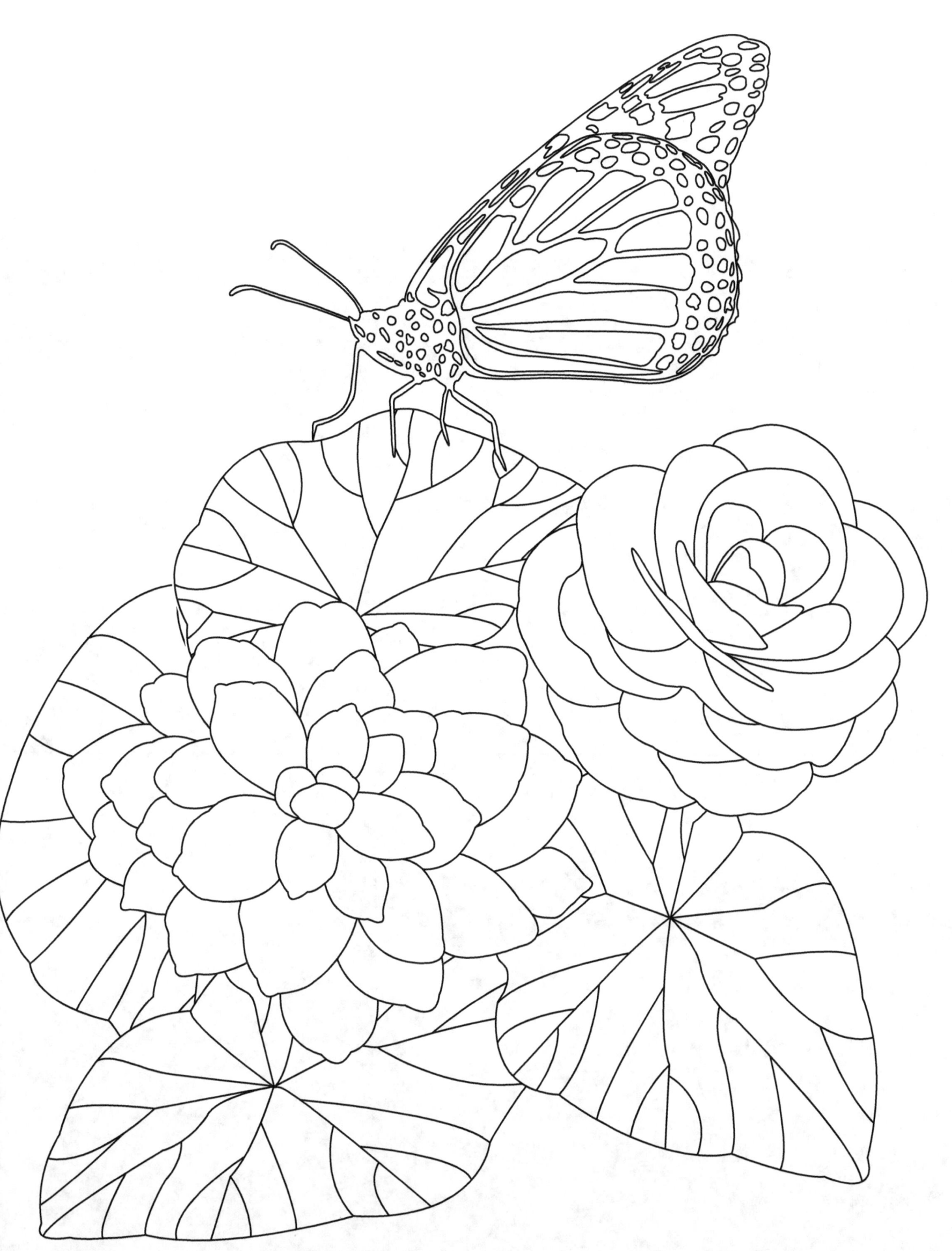

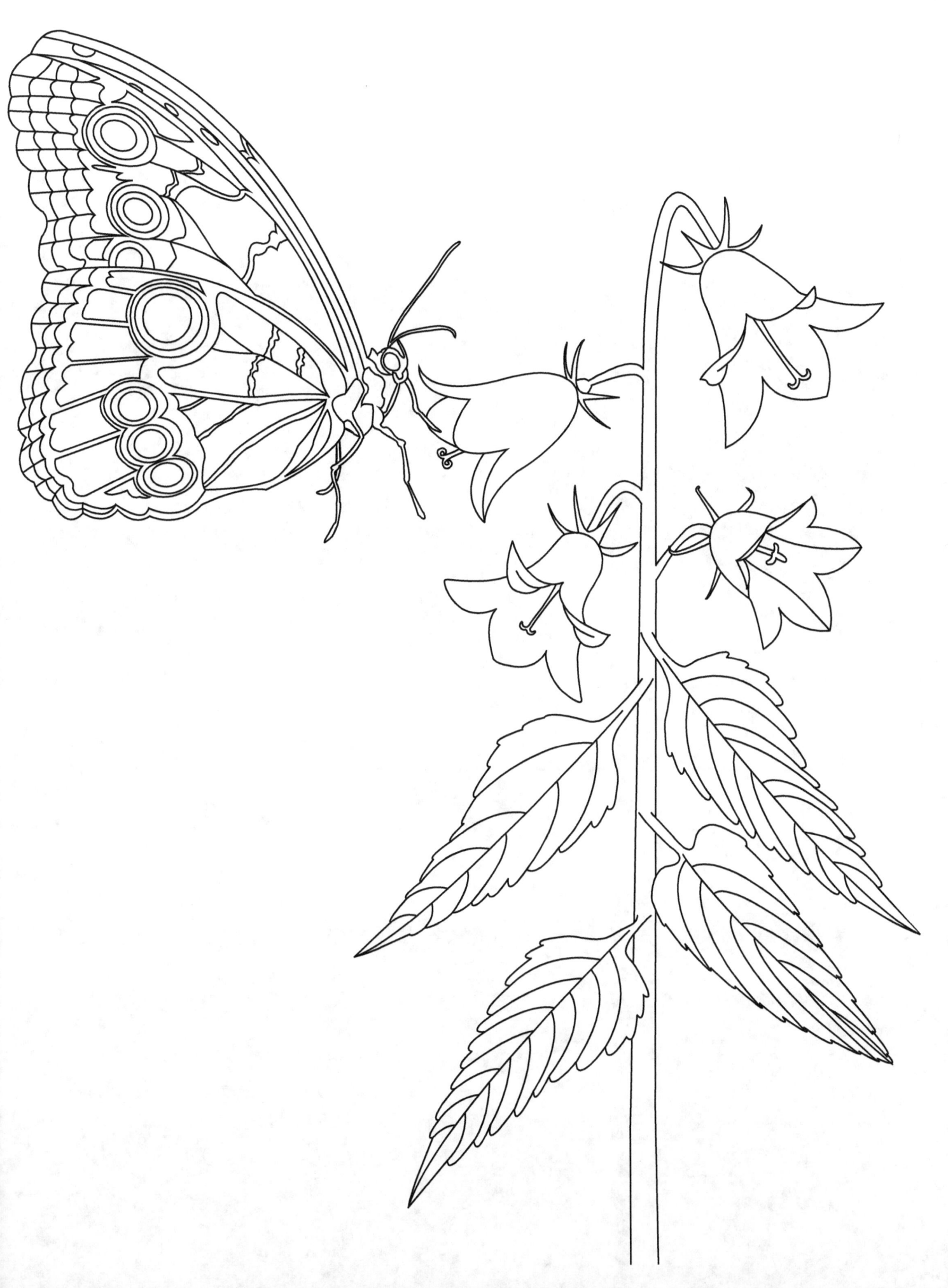

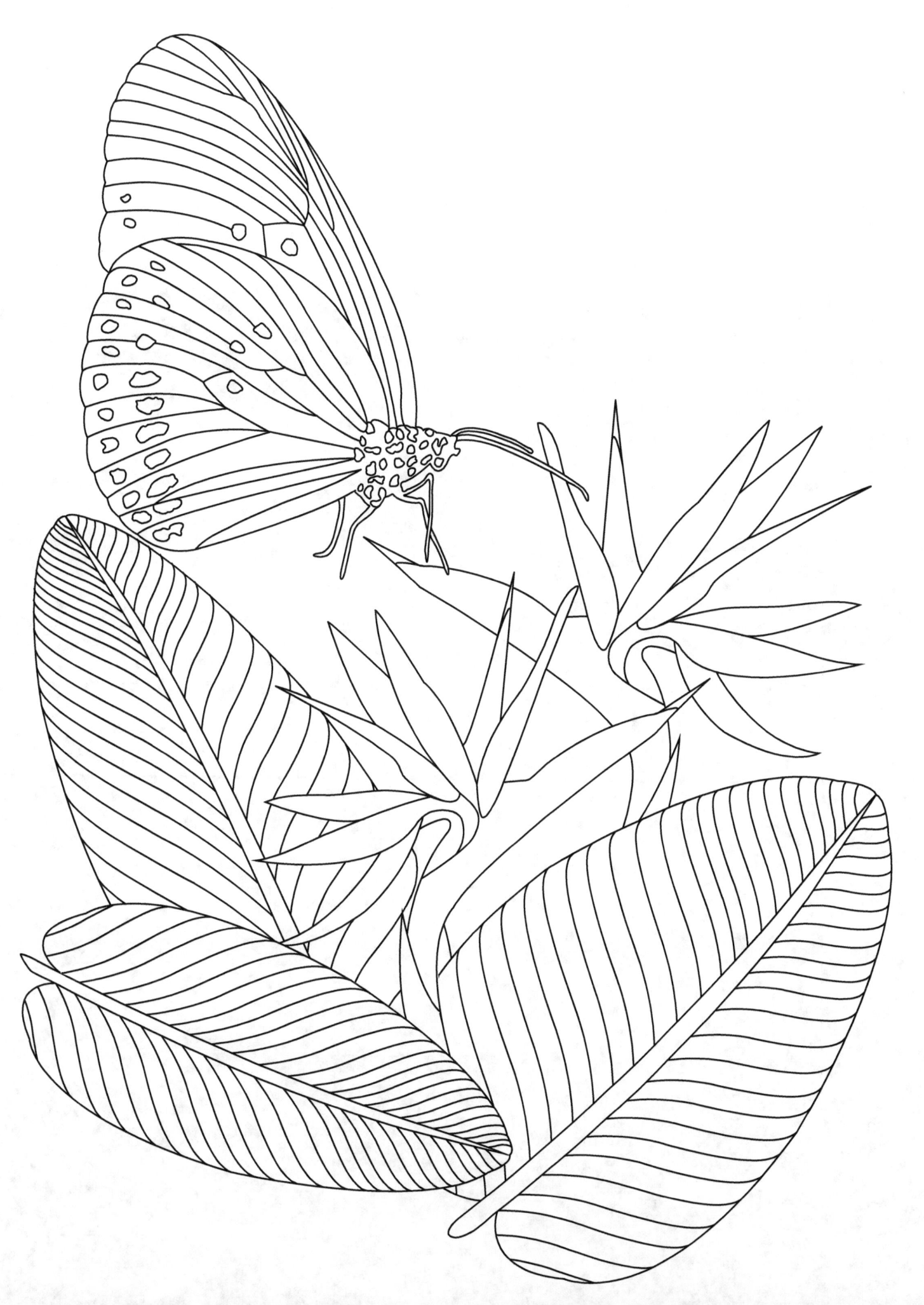

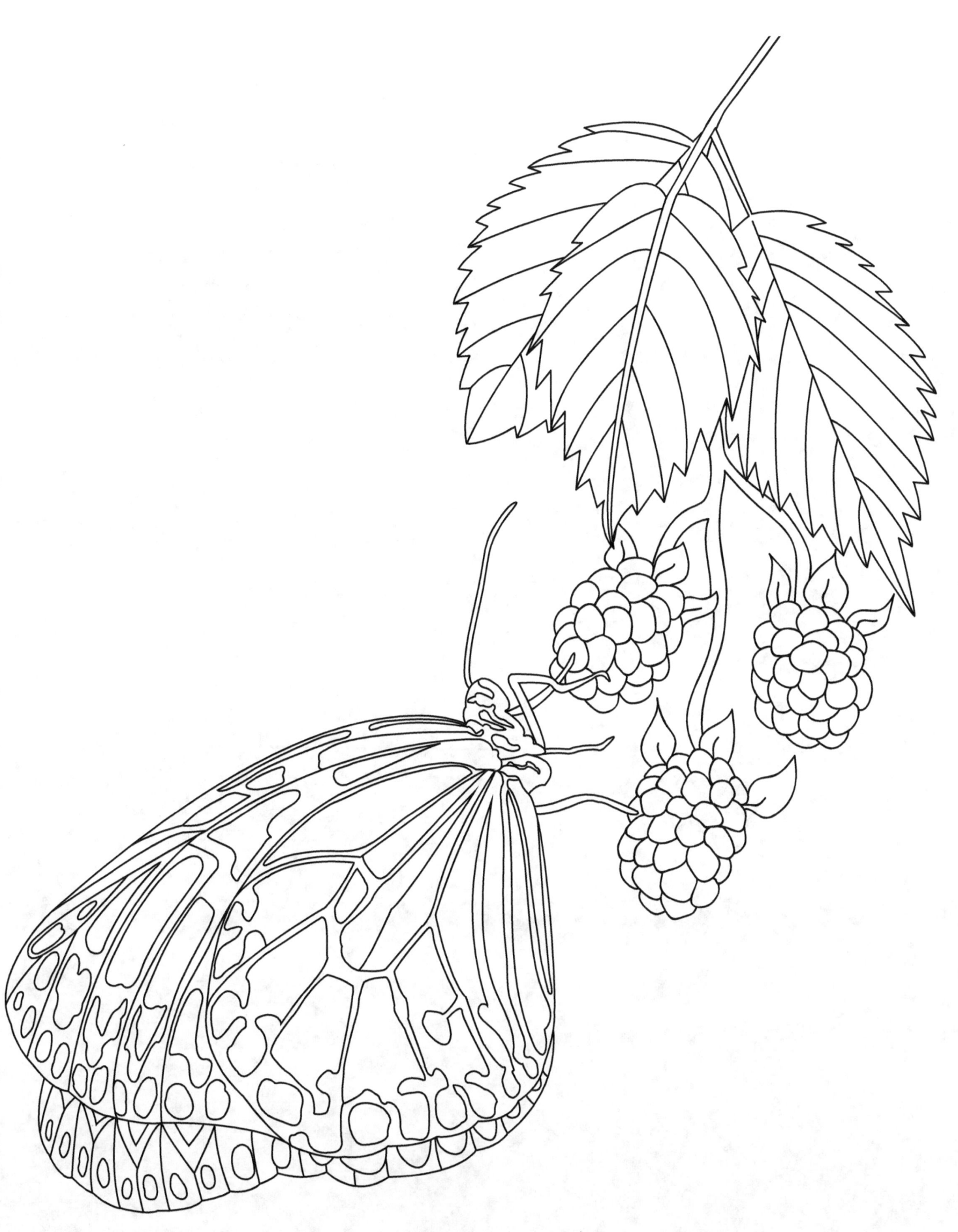

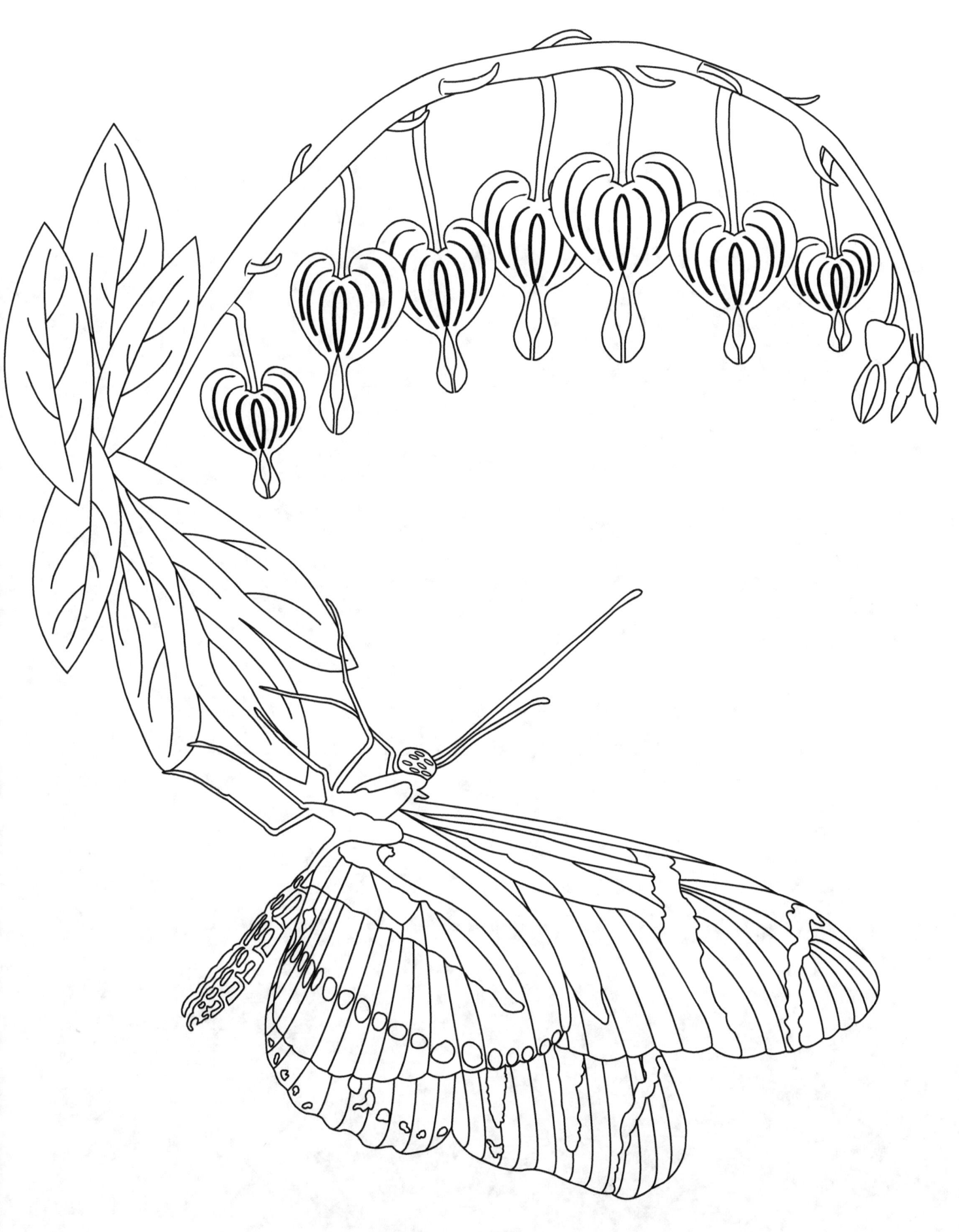

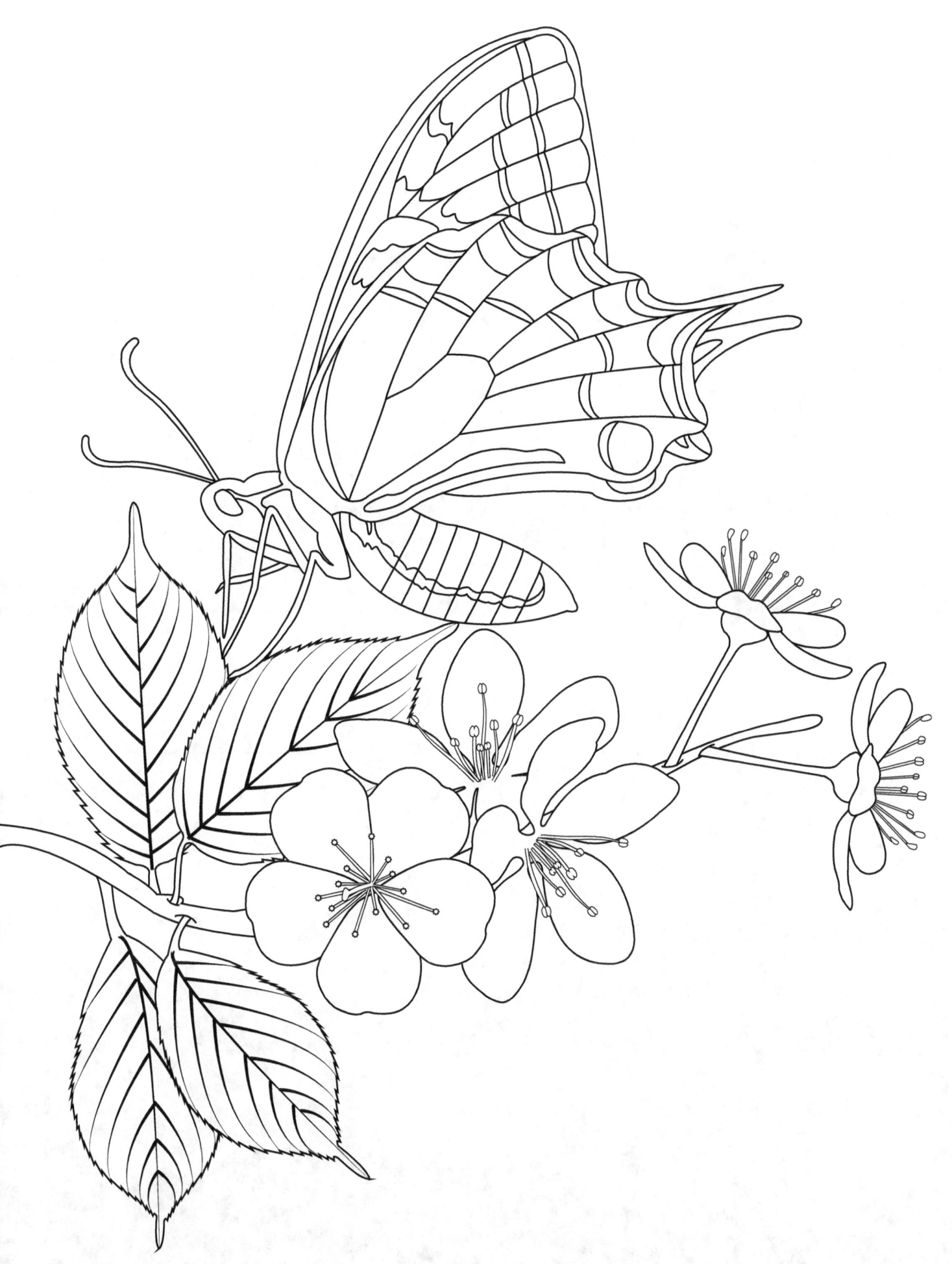

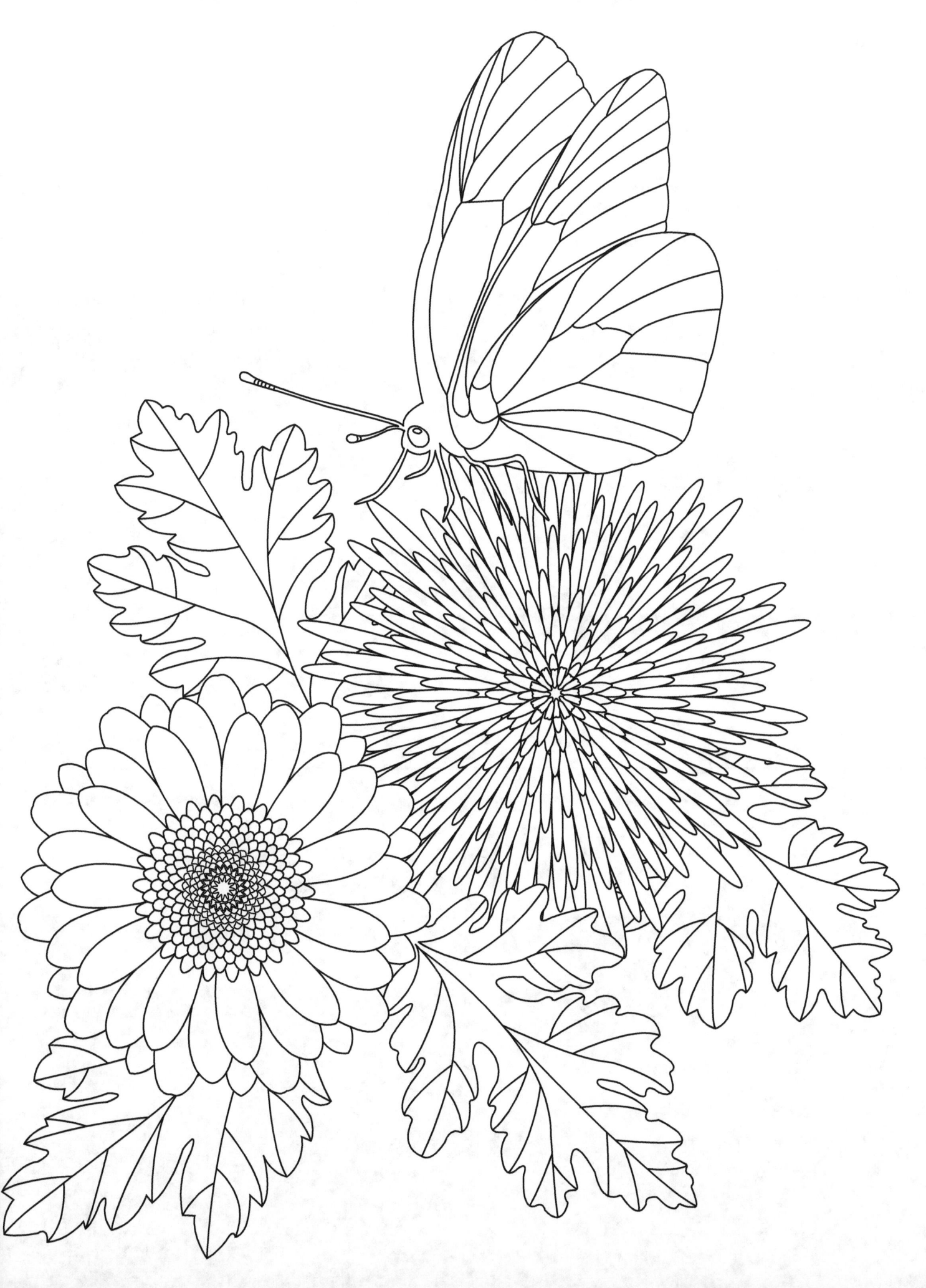

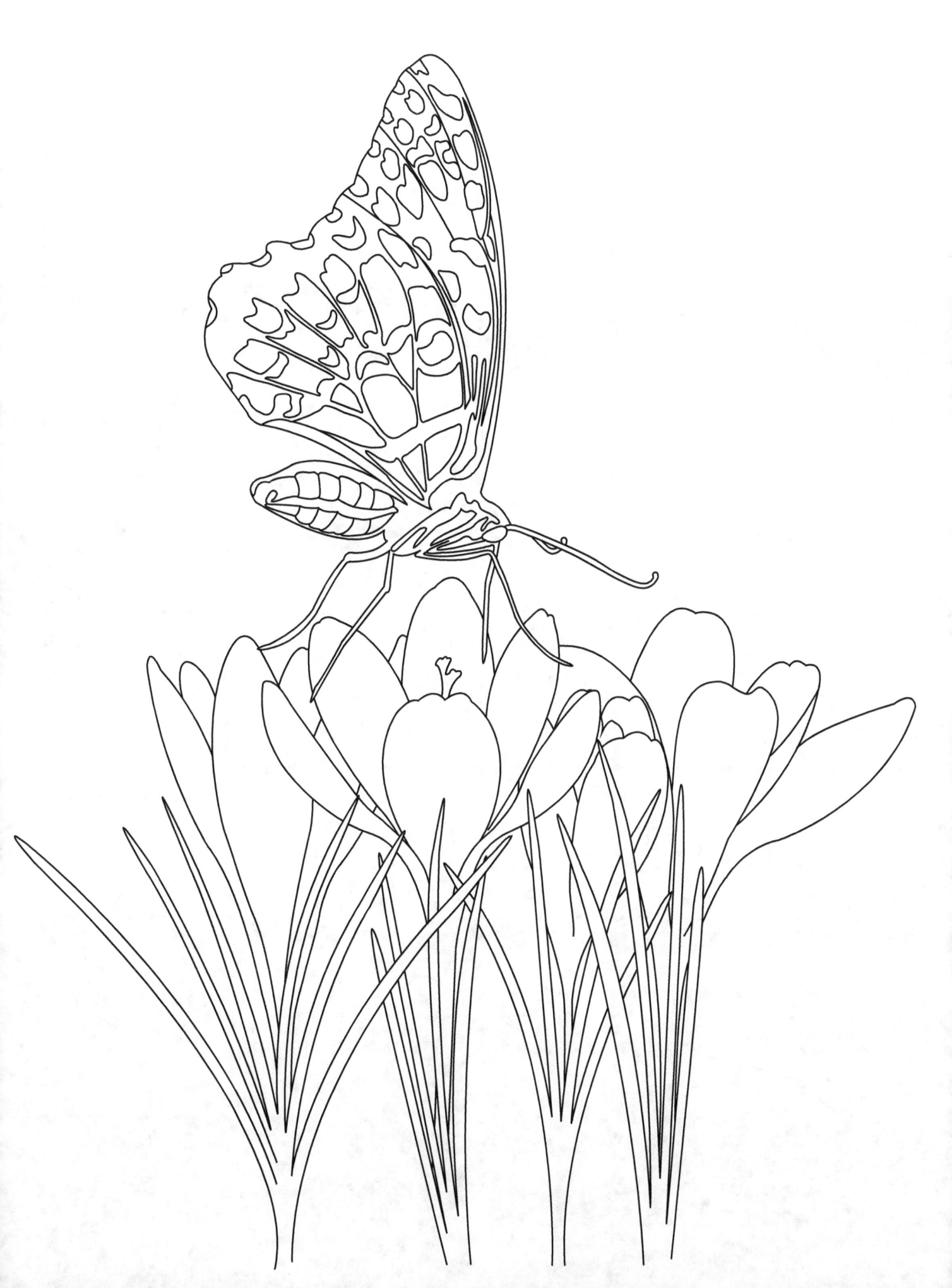

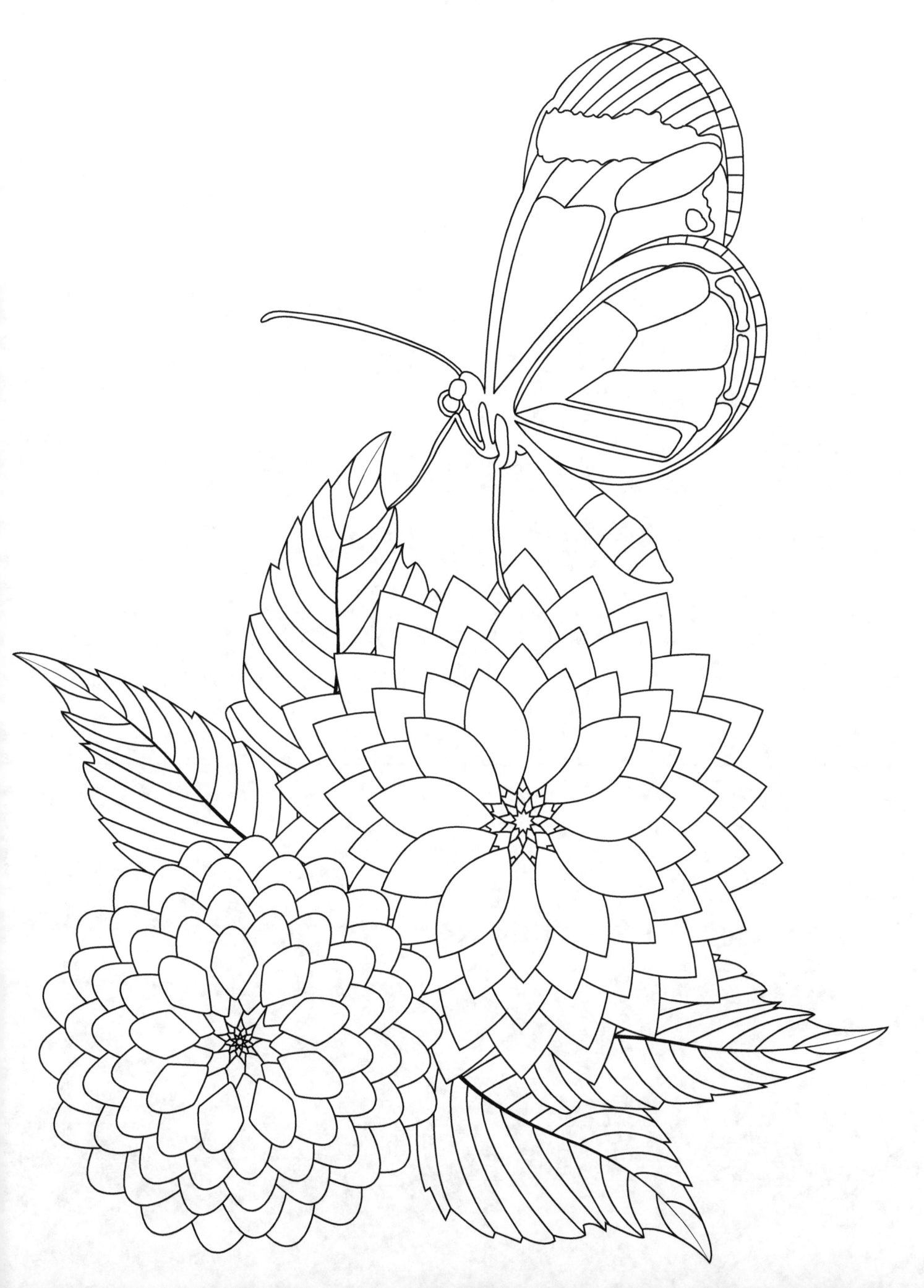

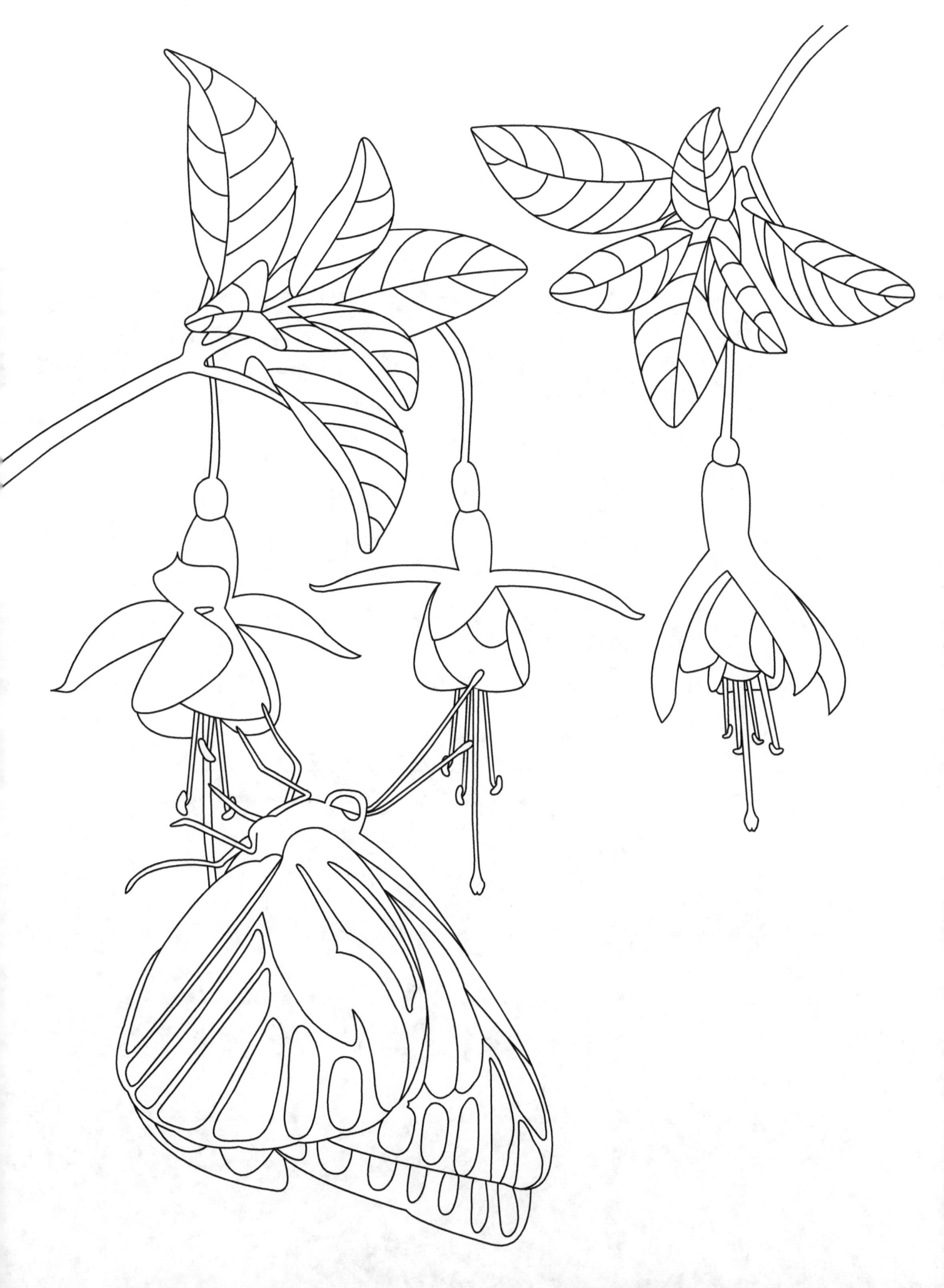

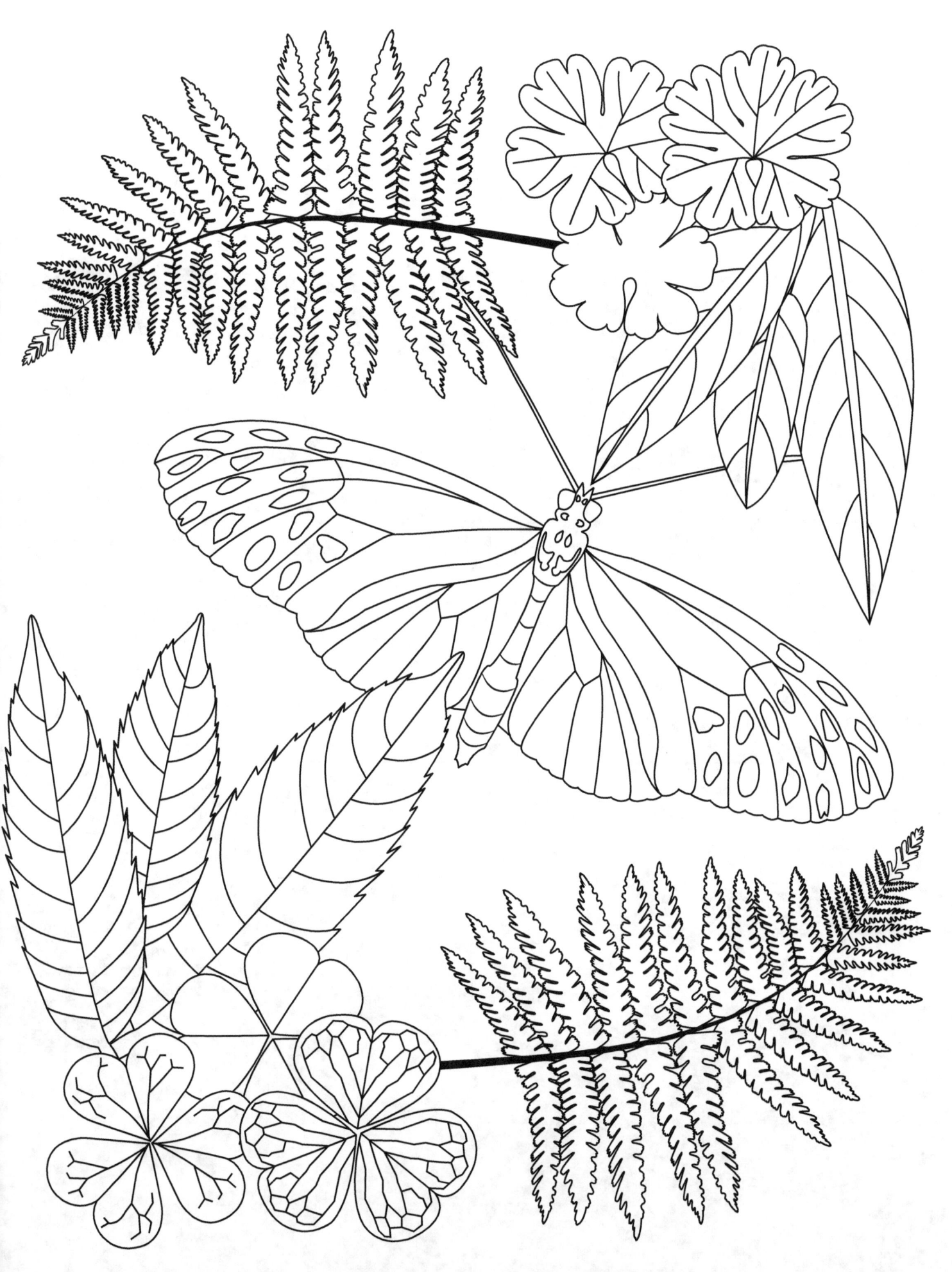

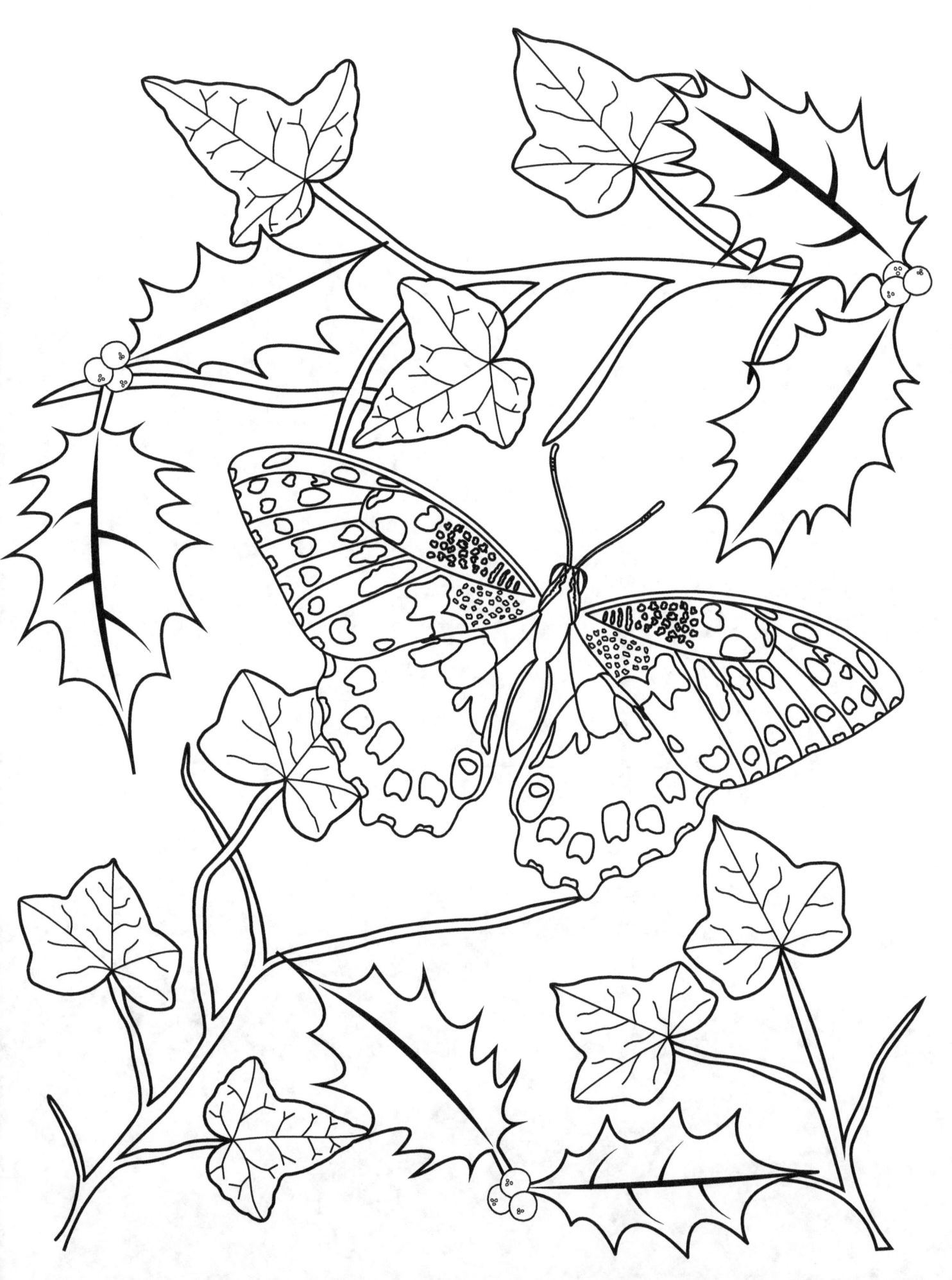

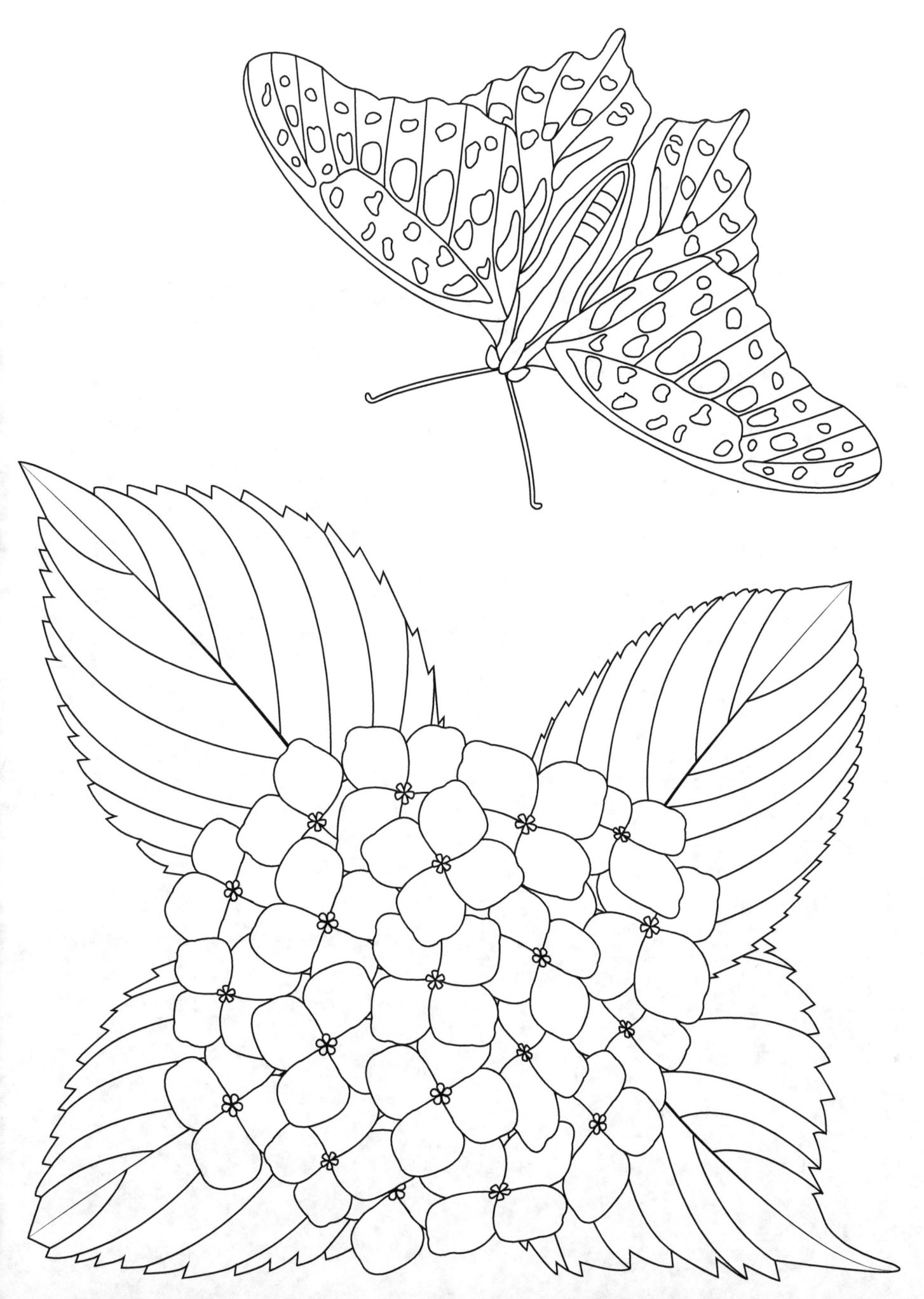

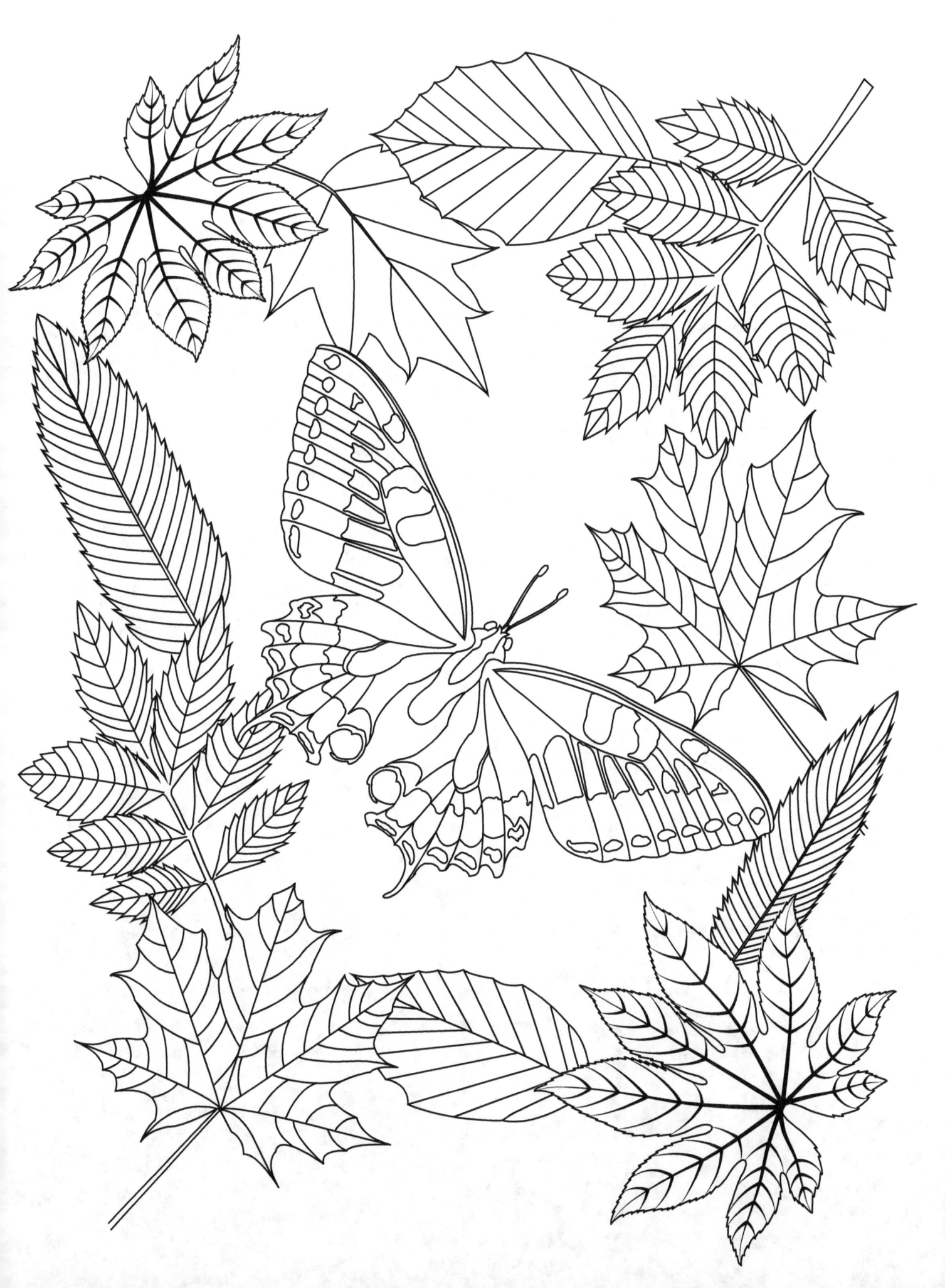

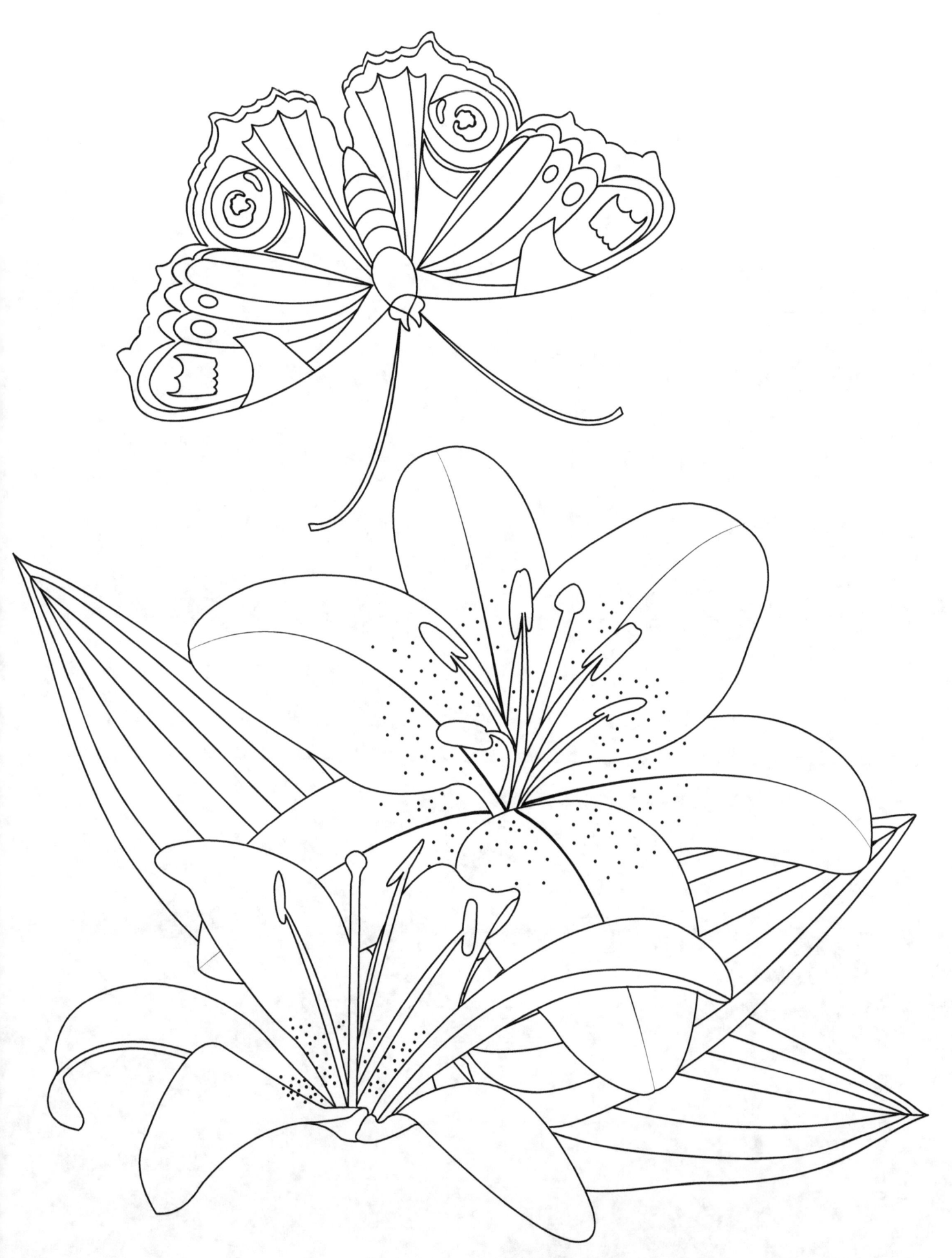

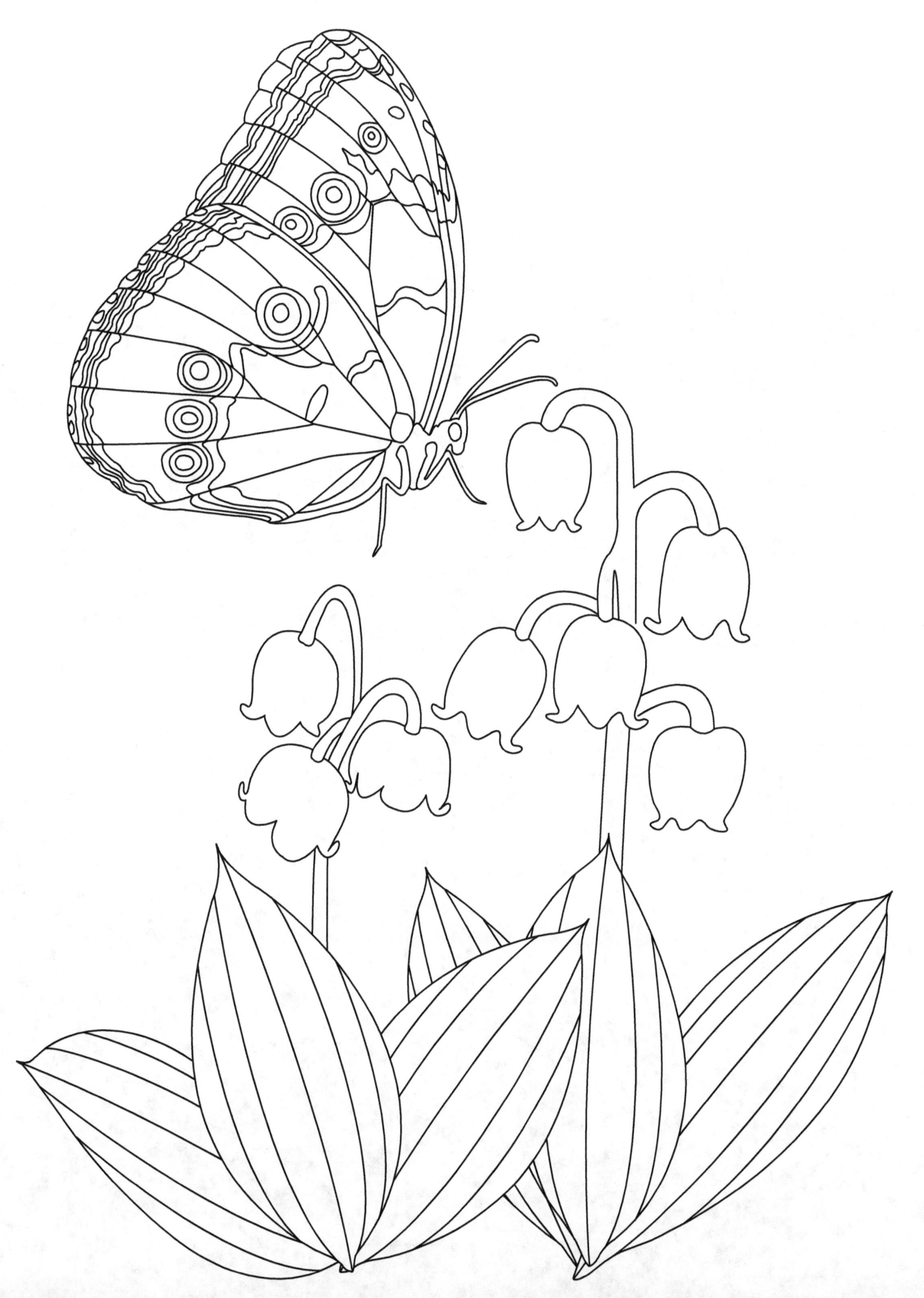

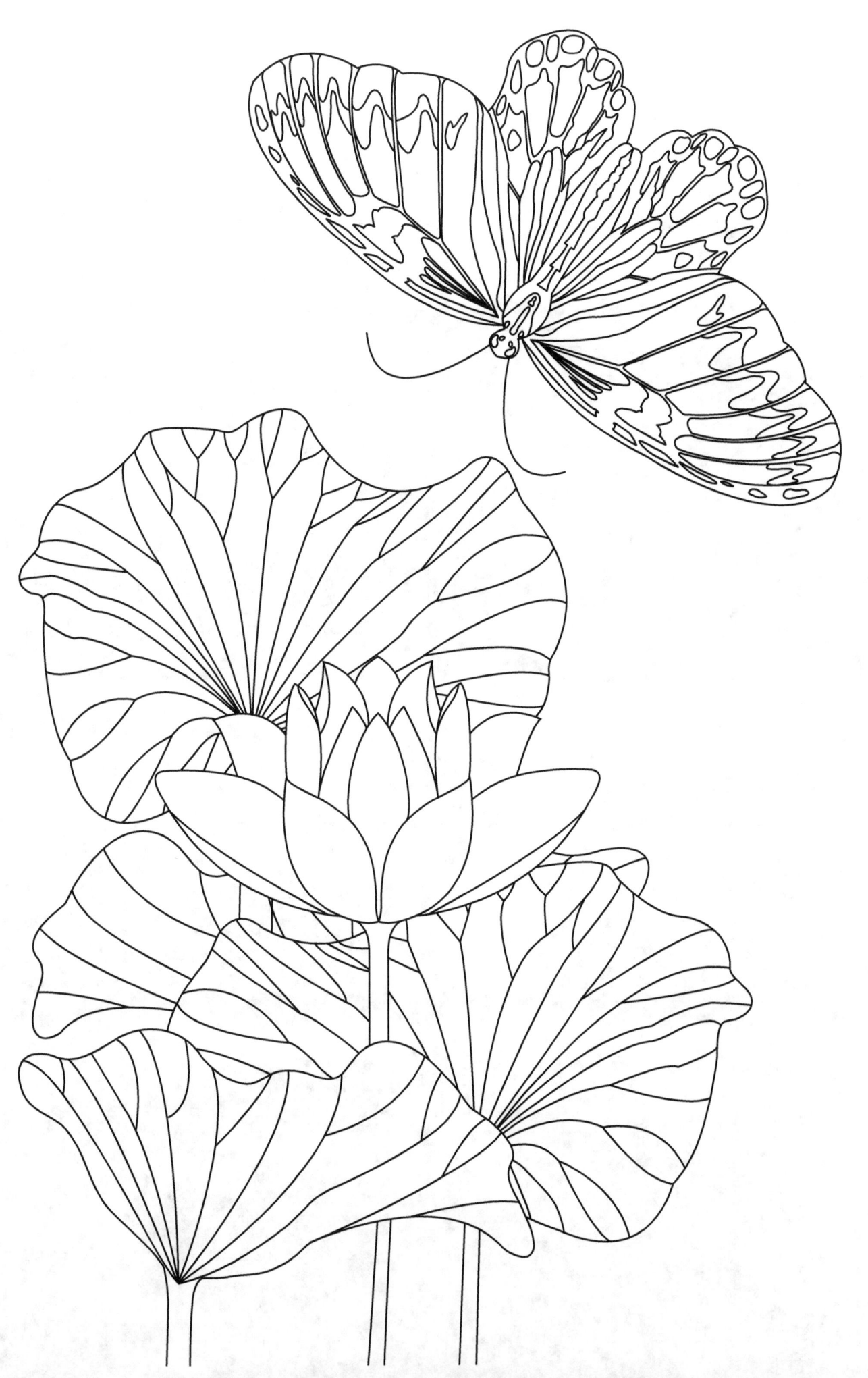

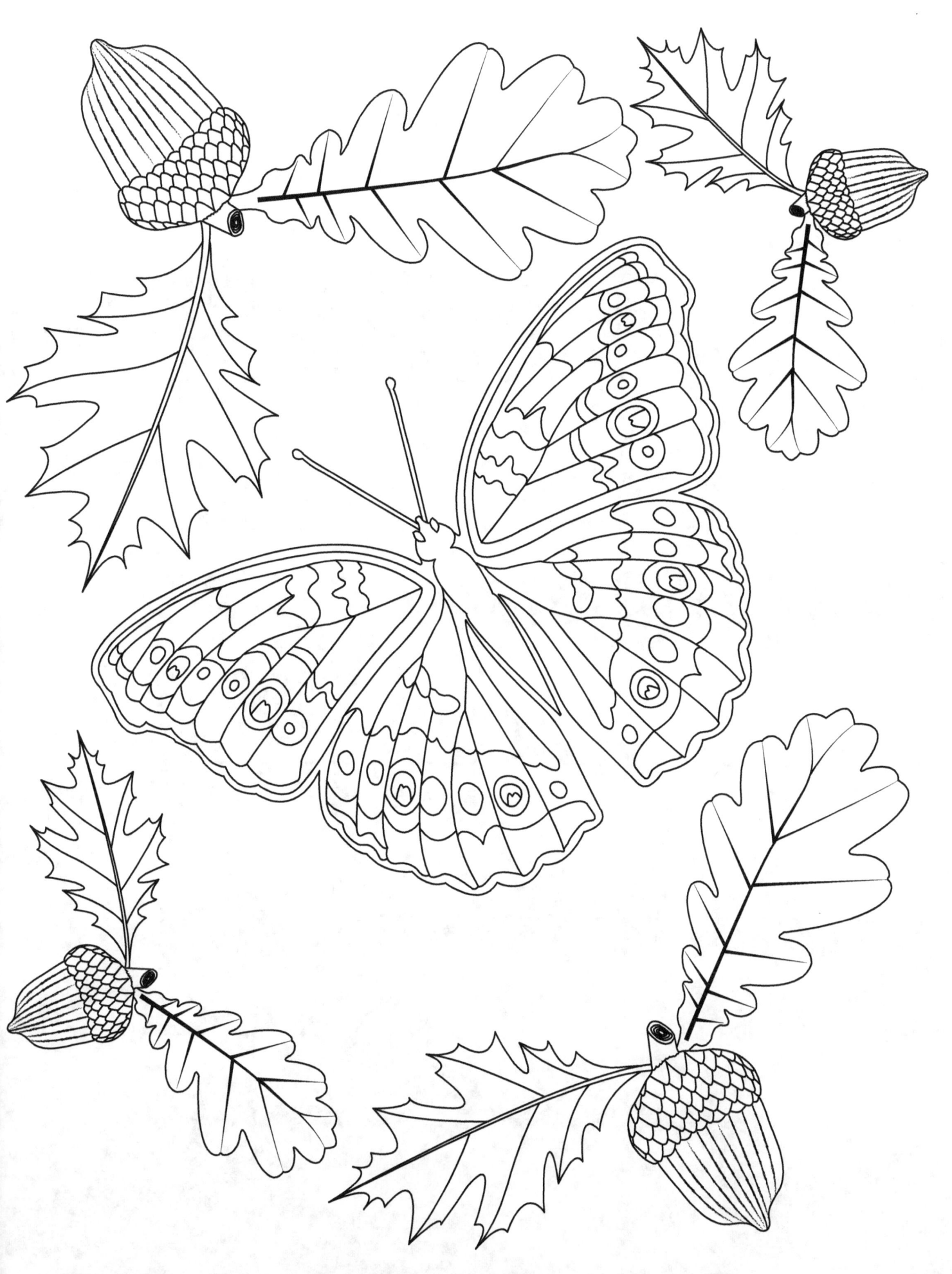

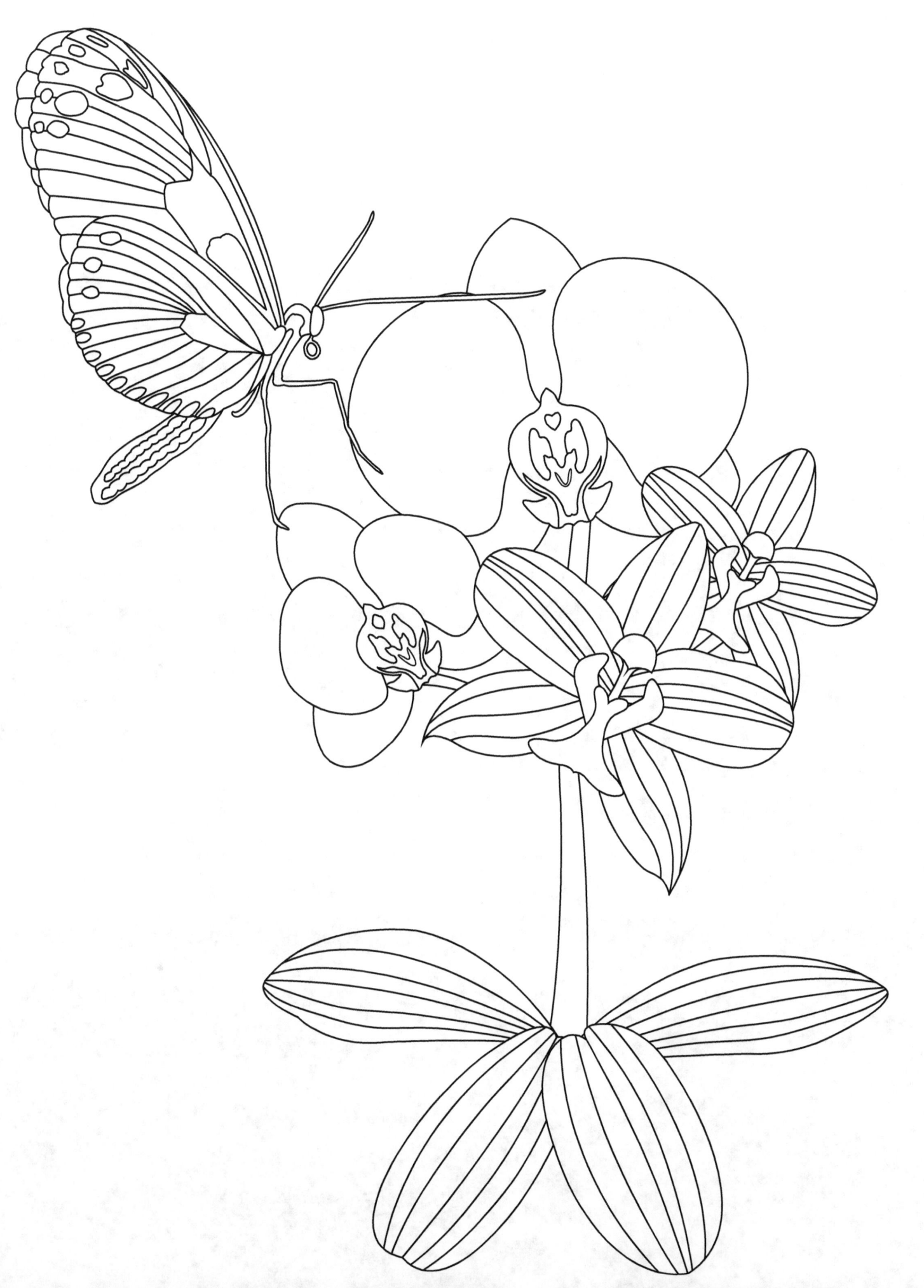

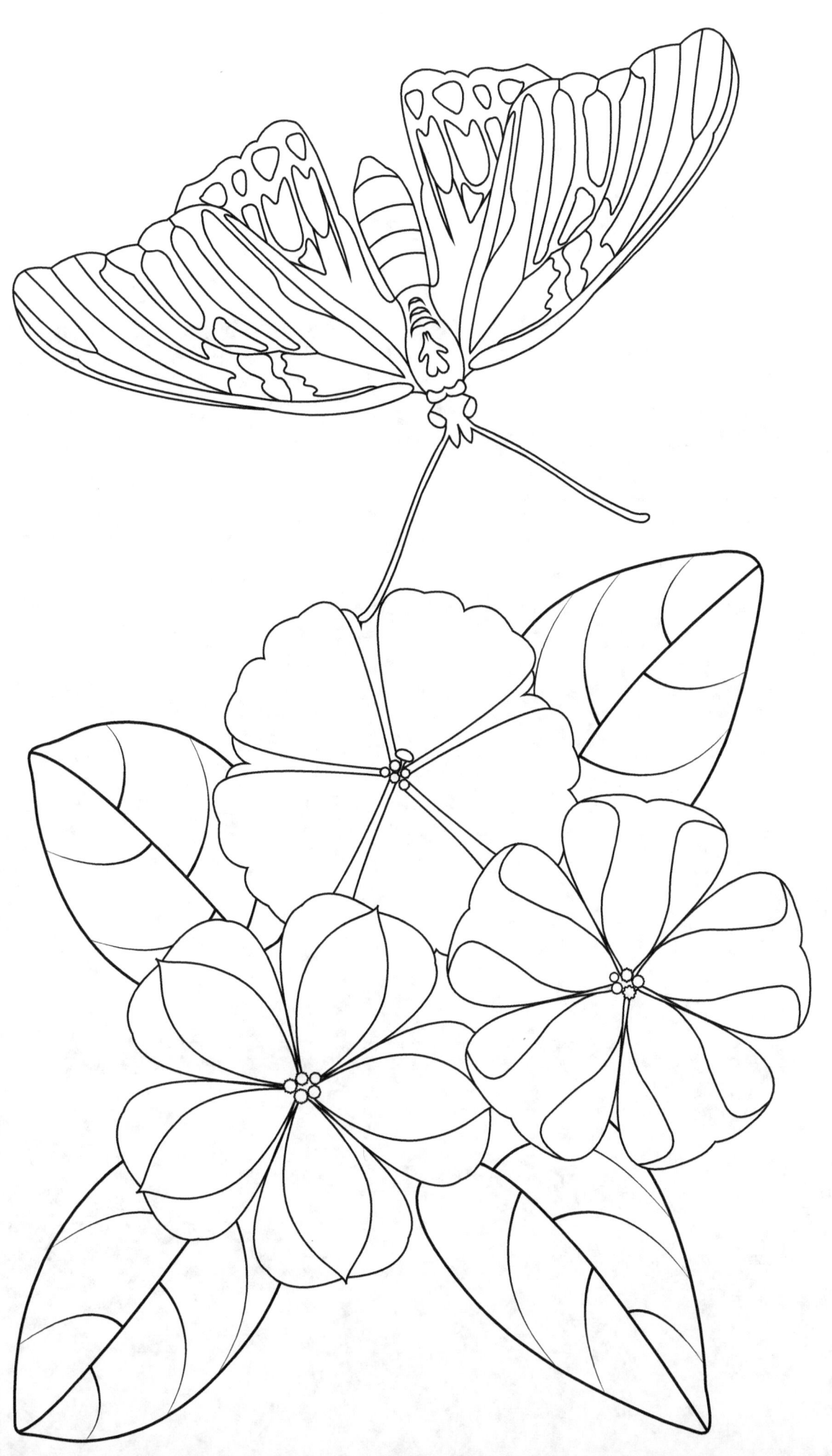

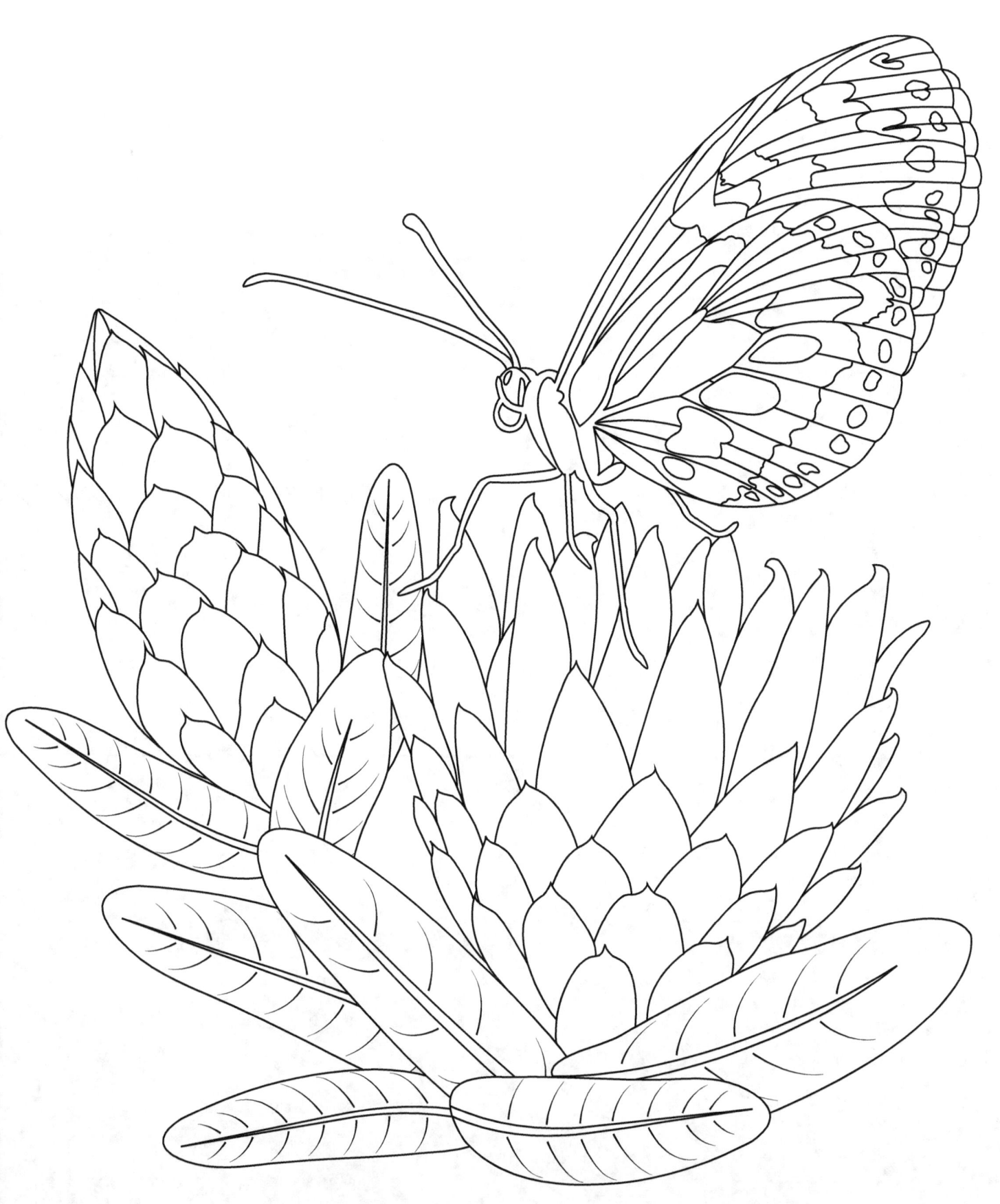

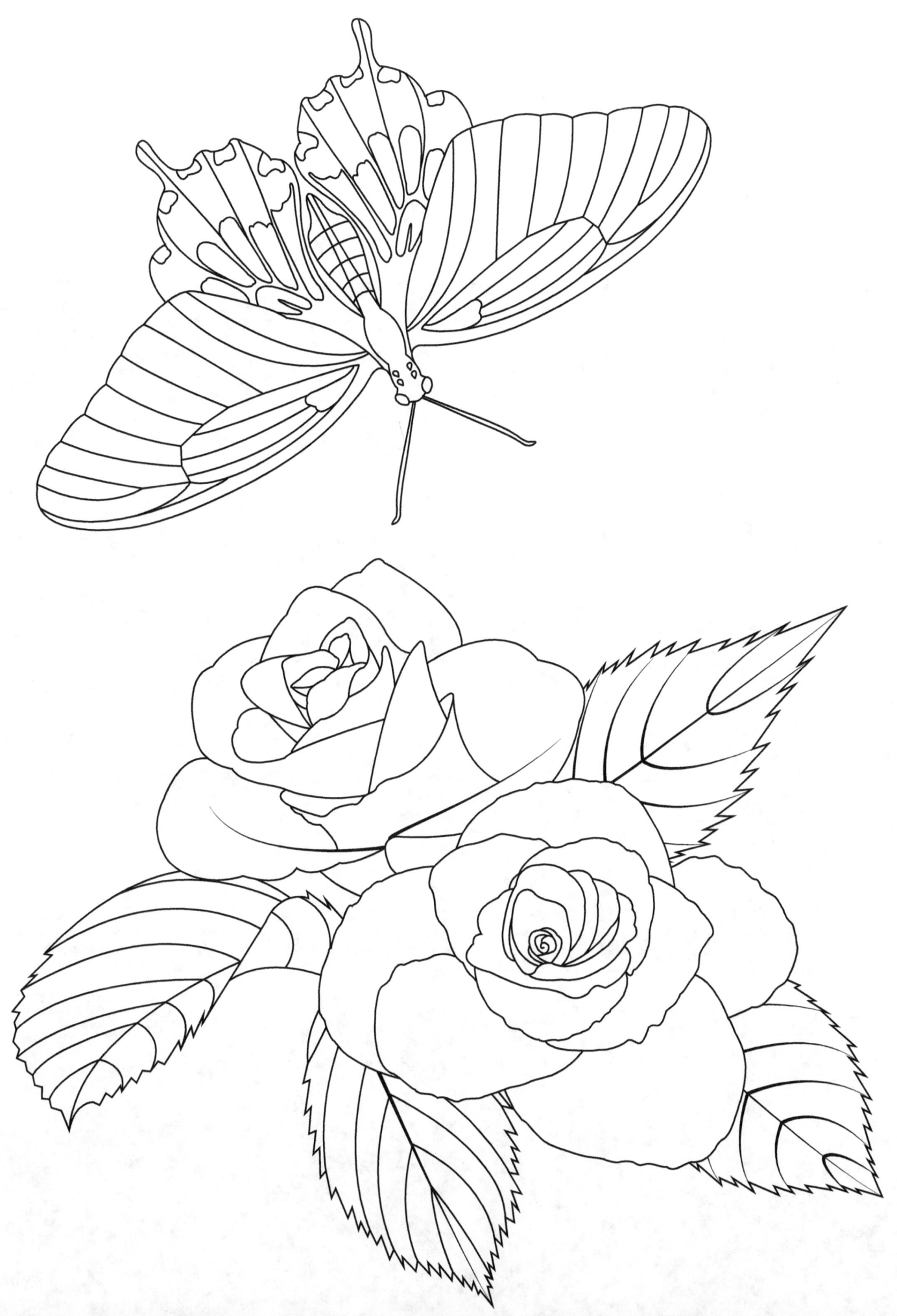

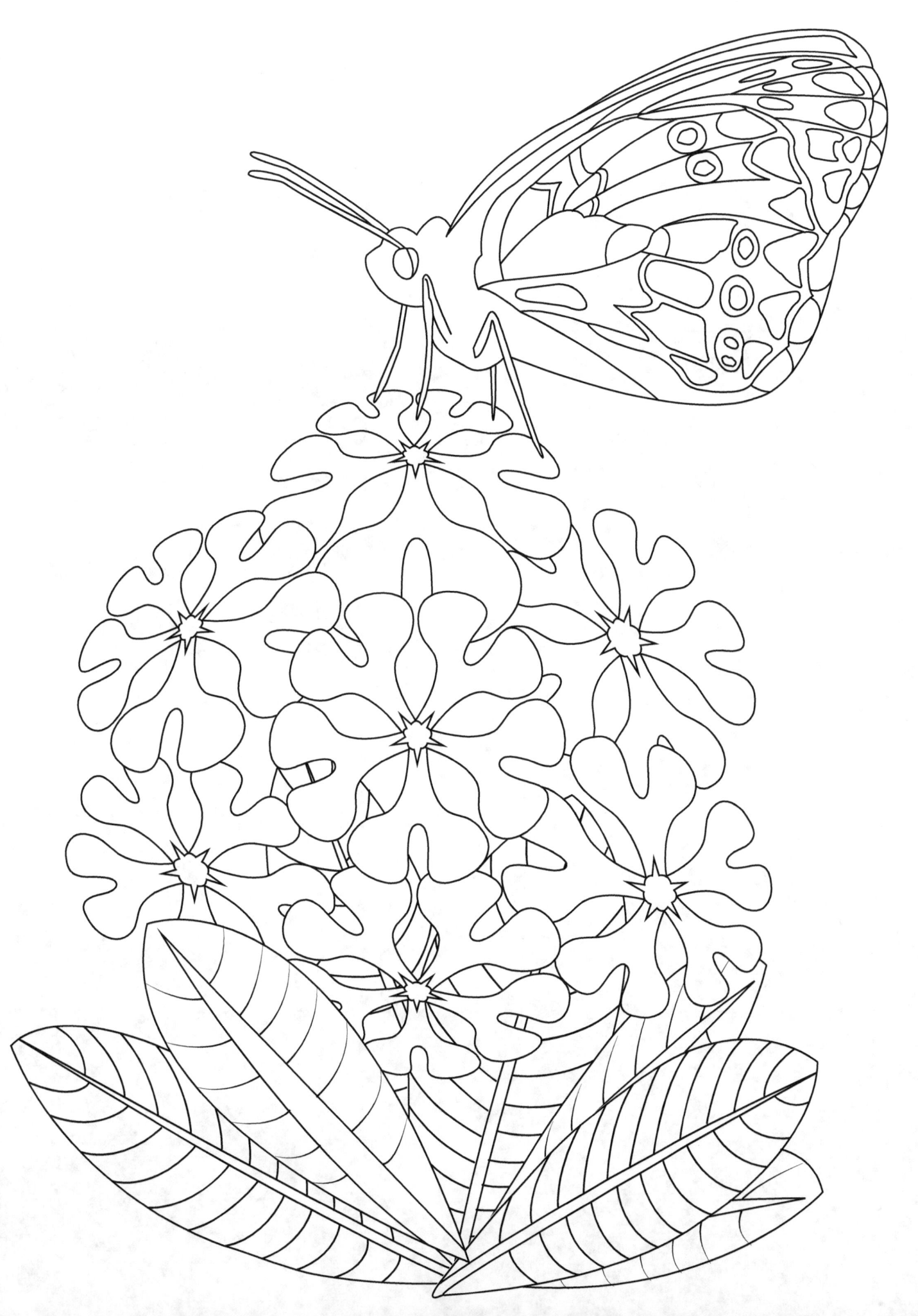

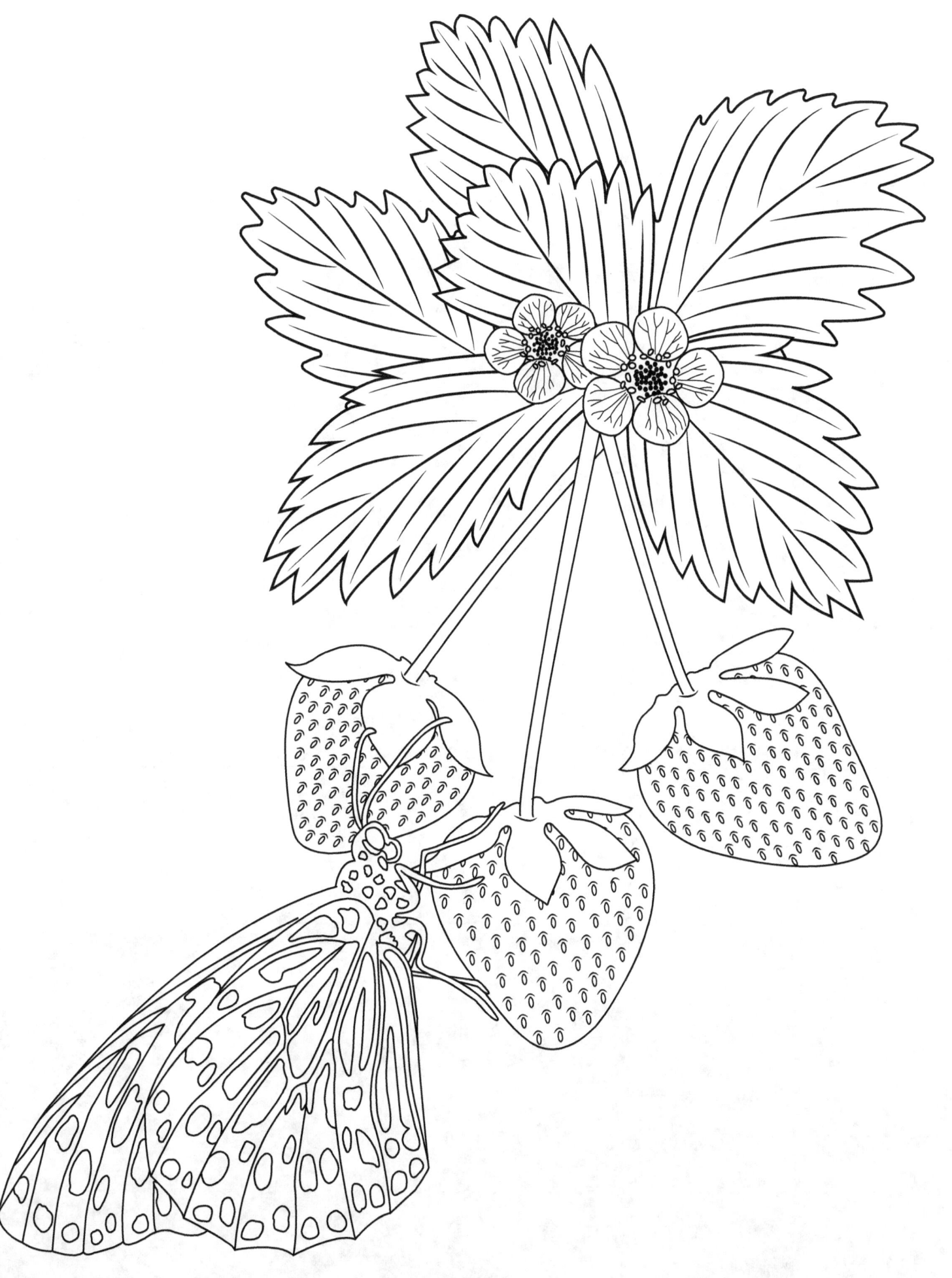

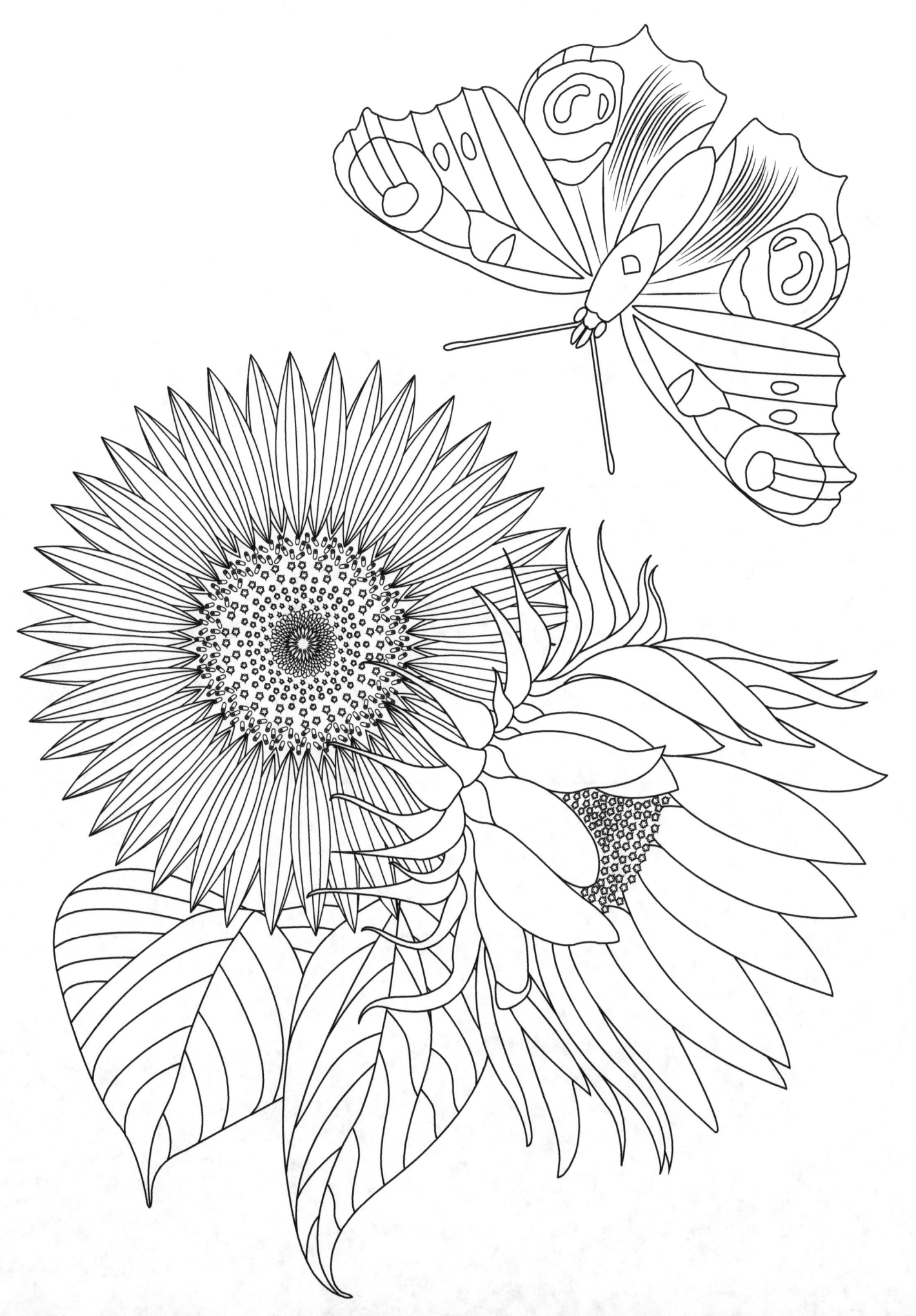

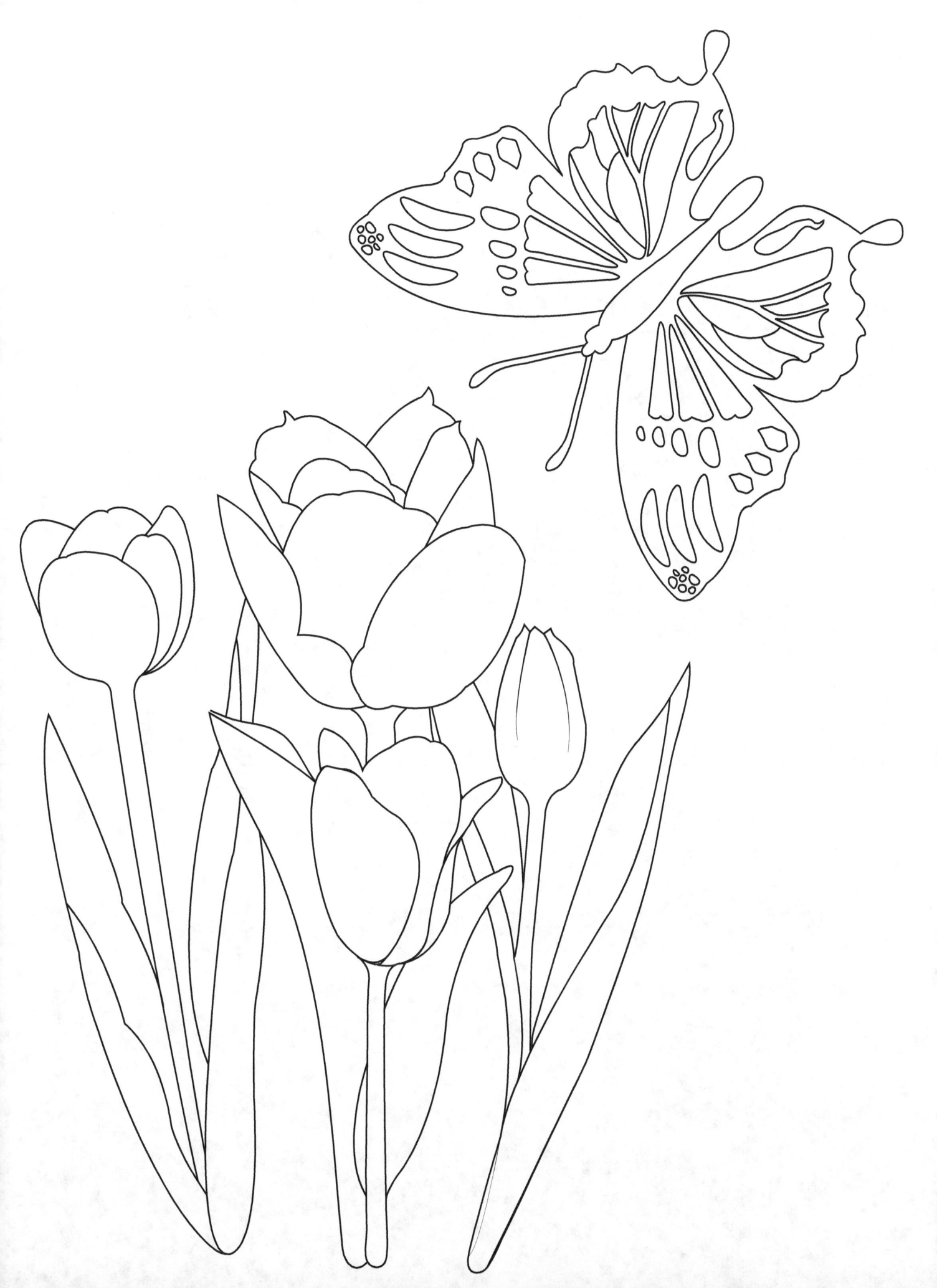

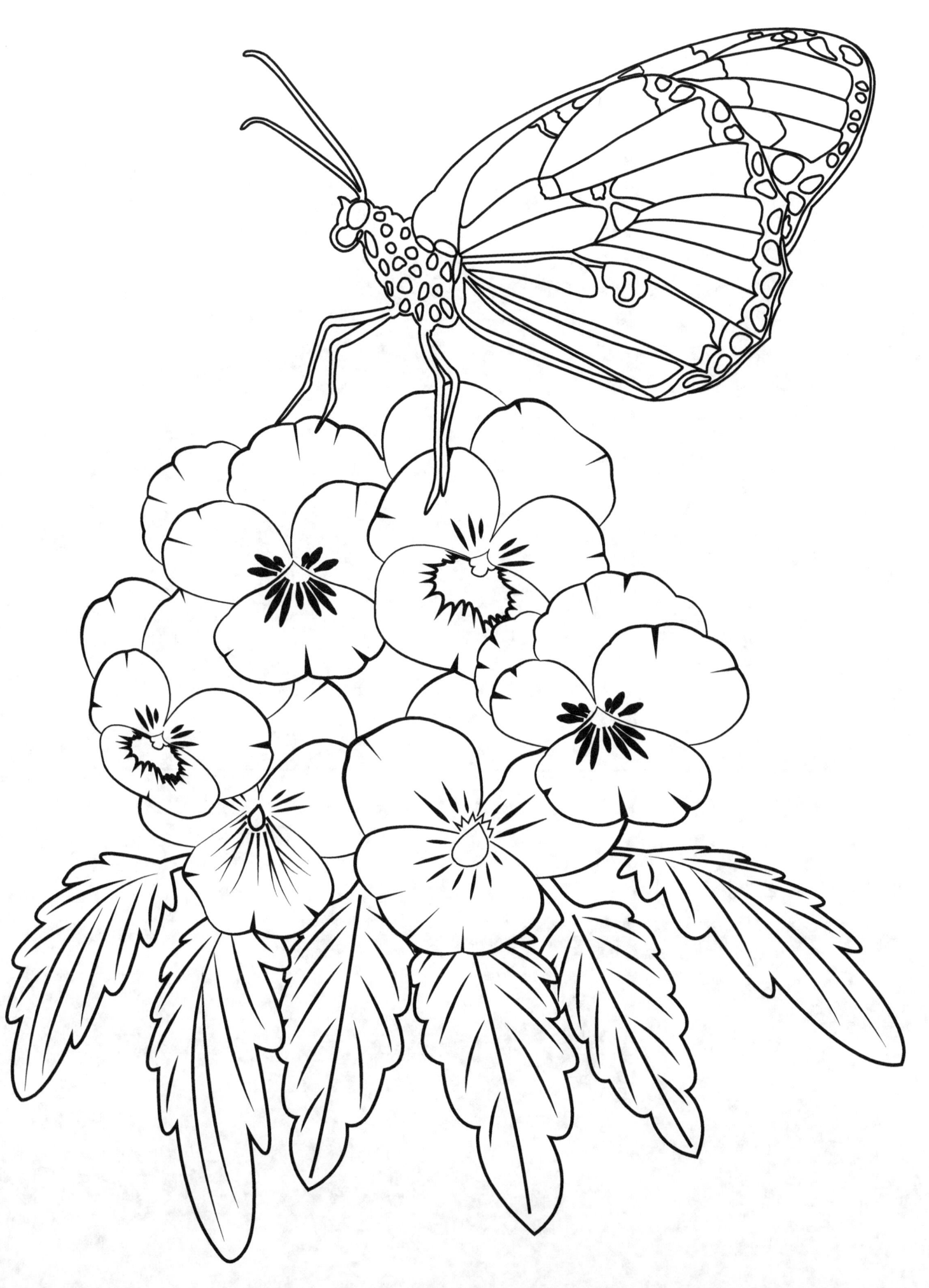

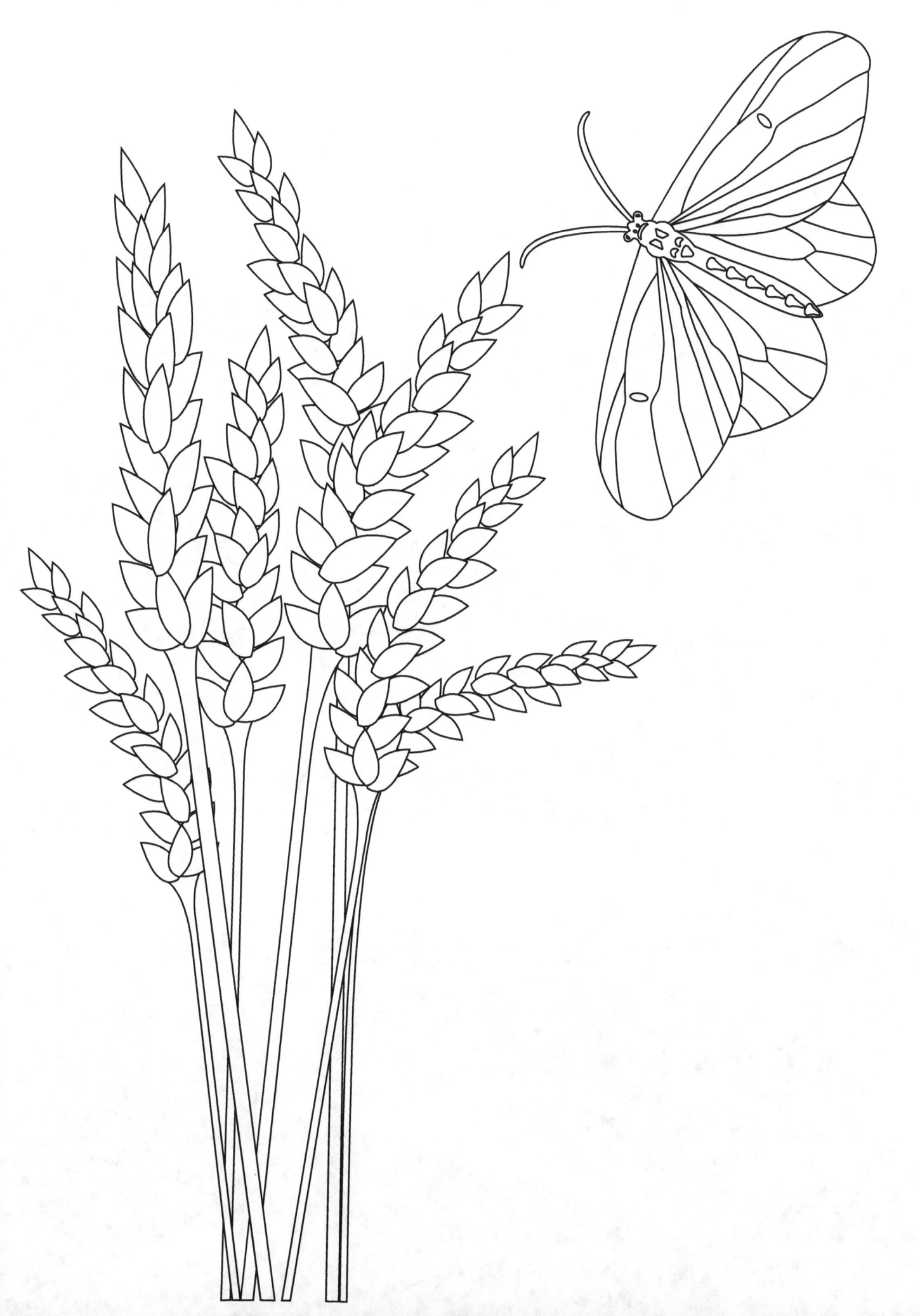

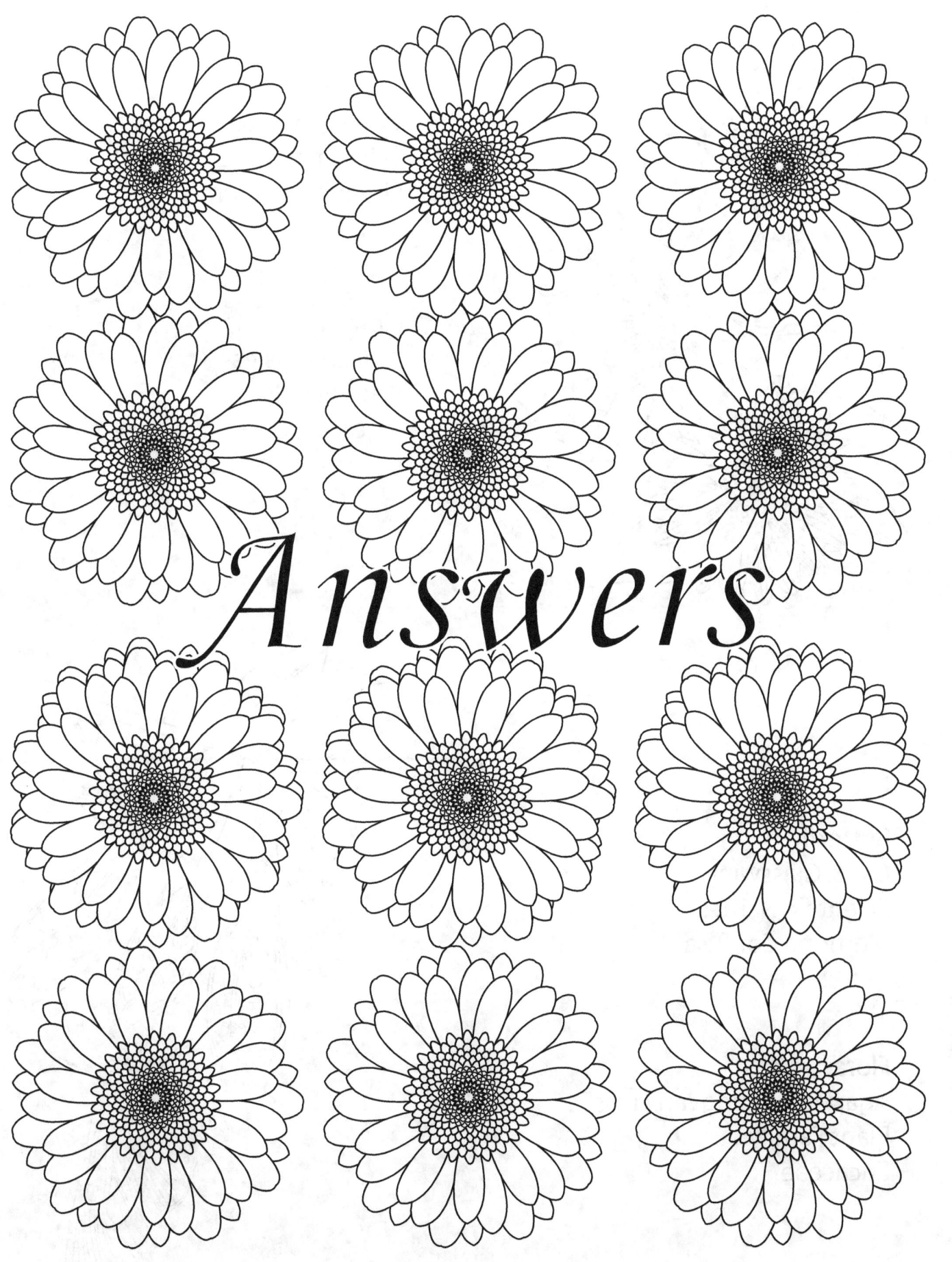

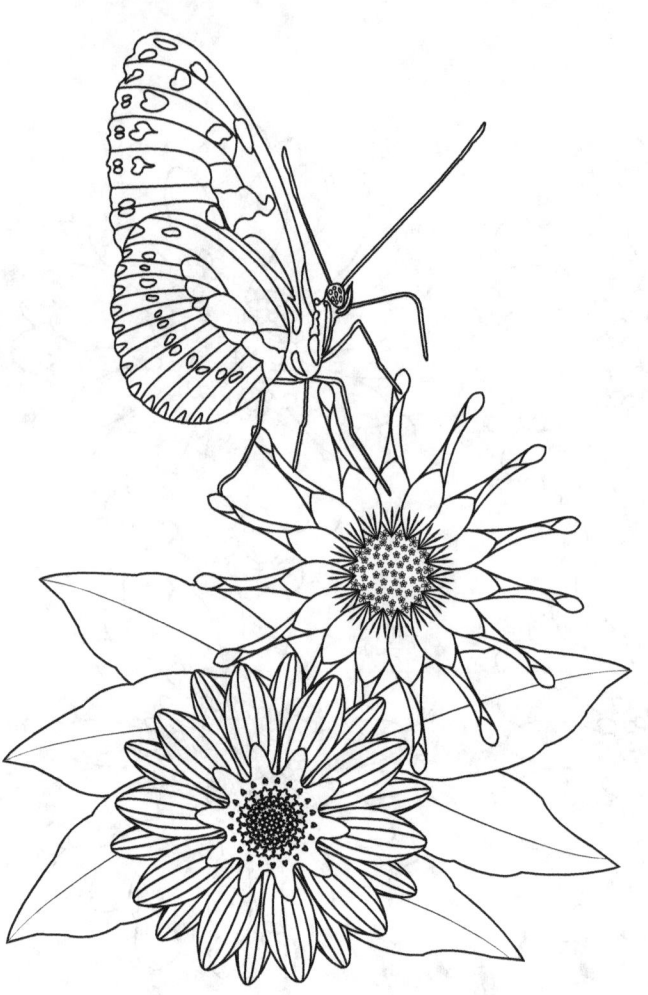

Butterfly:
White Admiral
Scientific Name:
Limenitis Arthemis

Flora:
African Daisies
Plant Family:
Asteraceae

Butterfly:
Giant Glasswing
Scientific Name:
Methona Confusa

Flora:
Agapetes "Ludgvan cross"
Plant Family:
Ericaceae

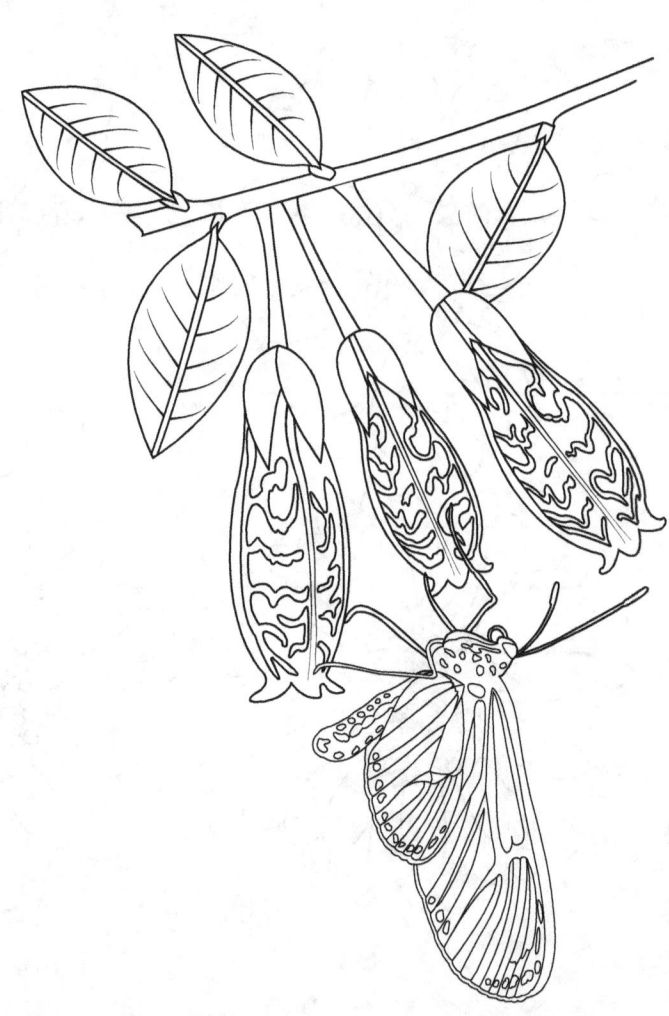

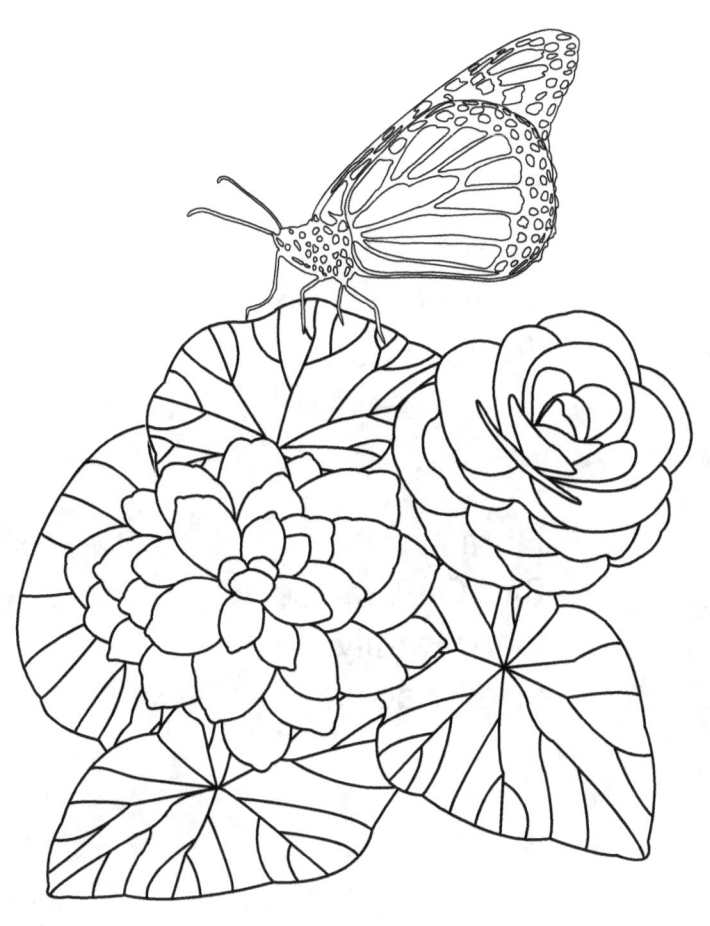

Butterfly:
Monarch
Scientific Name:
Danaus Plexippus

Flora:
Begonias
Plant Family:
Begoniaceae

Butterfly:
Morpho
Scientific Name:
Morpho Peleides

Flora:
Bellflower Campanula
Campanulaceae

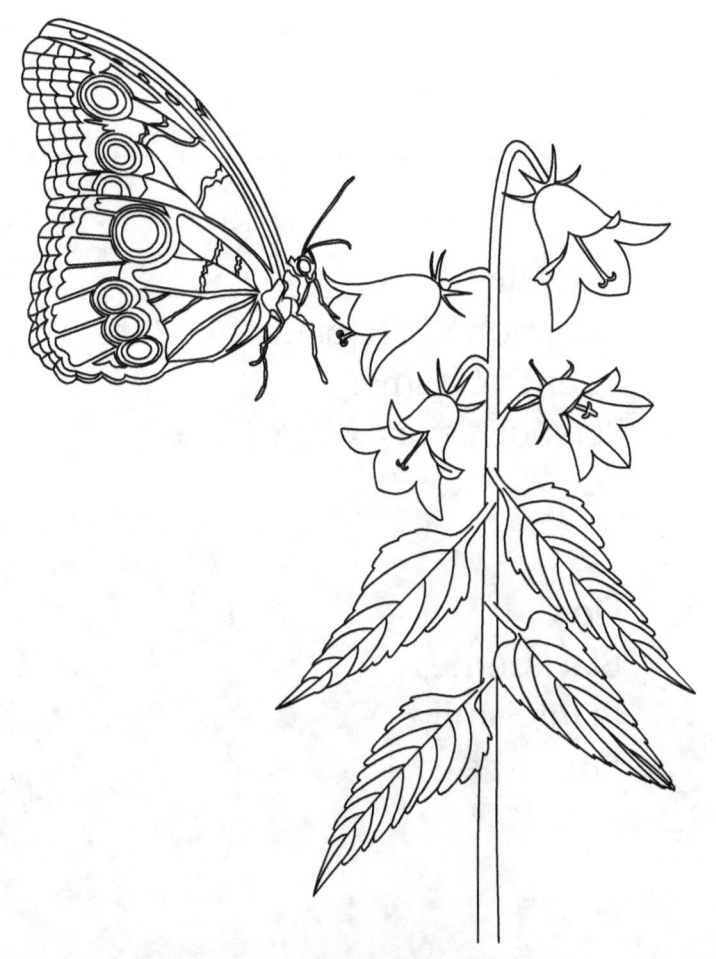

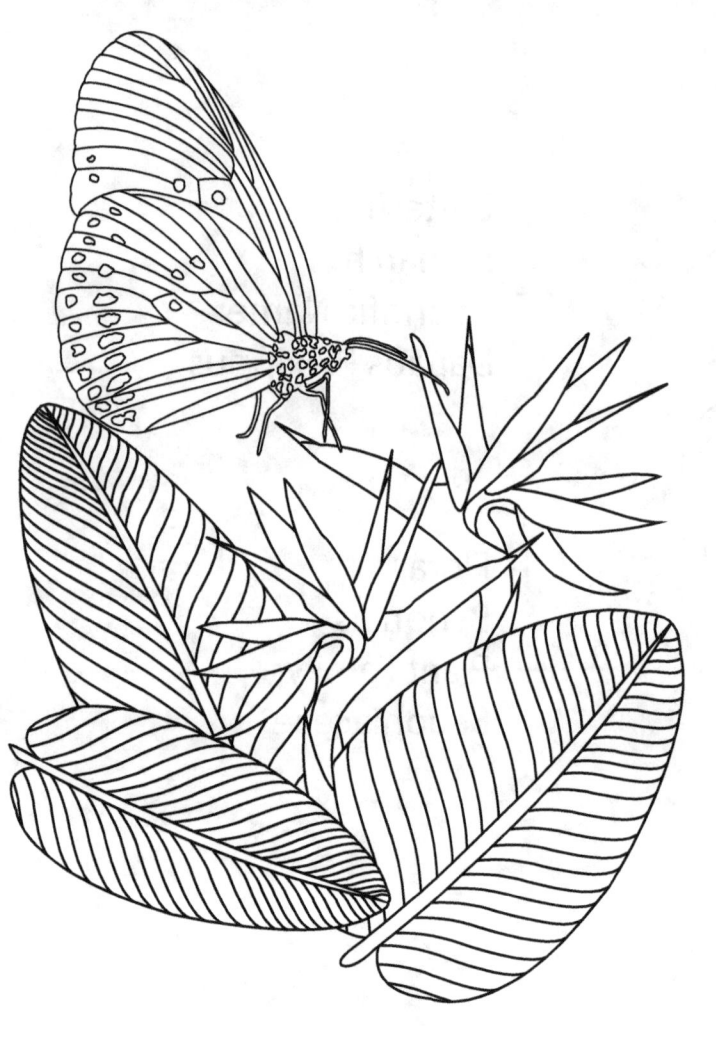

Butterfly:
Common Crow
Scientific Name:
Euploea Core

Flora:
Bird Of Paradise
Plant Family:
Strelitziaceae

Butterfly:
Common White or Caper White
Scientific Name:
Belenois Java

Flora:
Blackberries
Plant Family:
Rosaceae

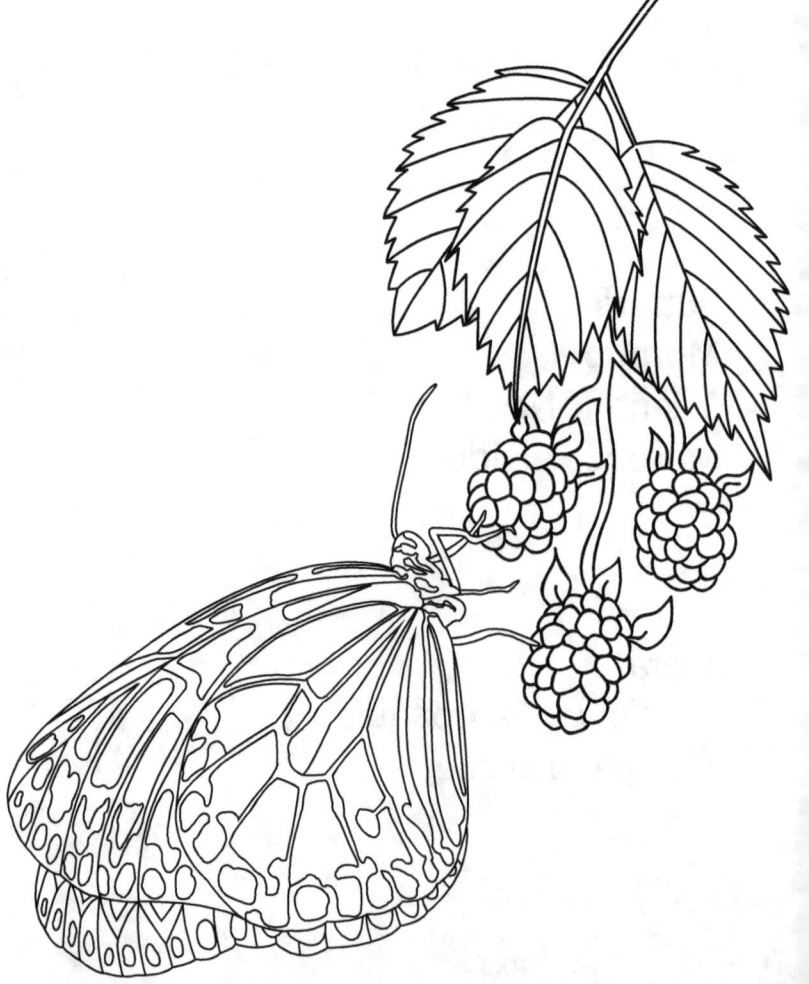

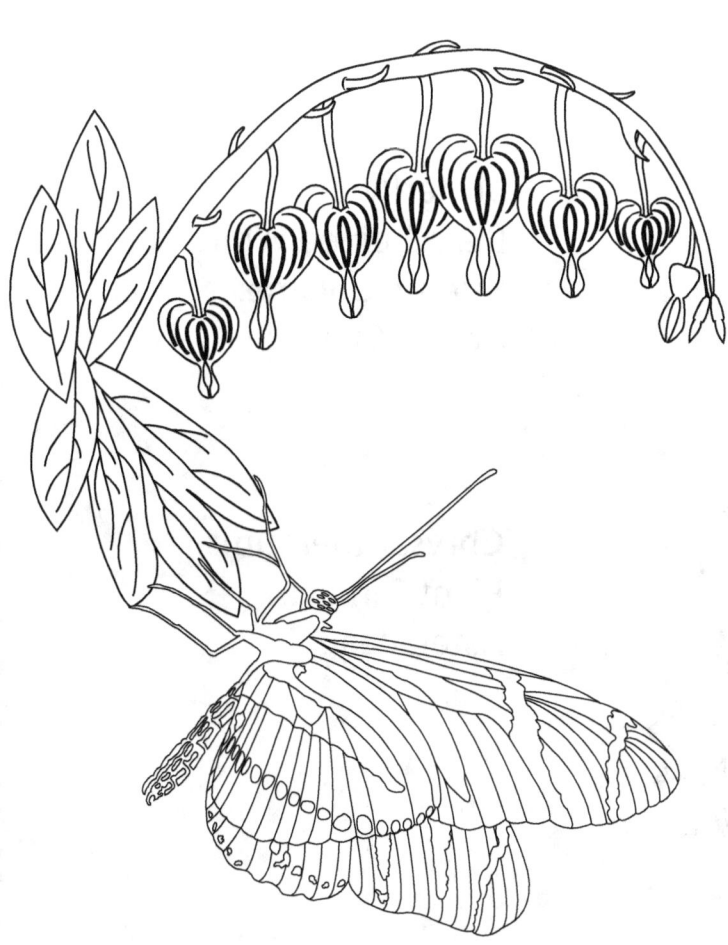

Butterfly:
Zebra Longwing or Heliconian
Scientific Name:
Heliconius Charithonia

Flora:
Bleeding Heart
Plant Family:
Papaveraceae

Butterfly:
Asian Swallowtail
Scientific Name:
Papilio Xuthus

Flora:
Cherry Blossom
Plant Family:
Rosaceae

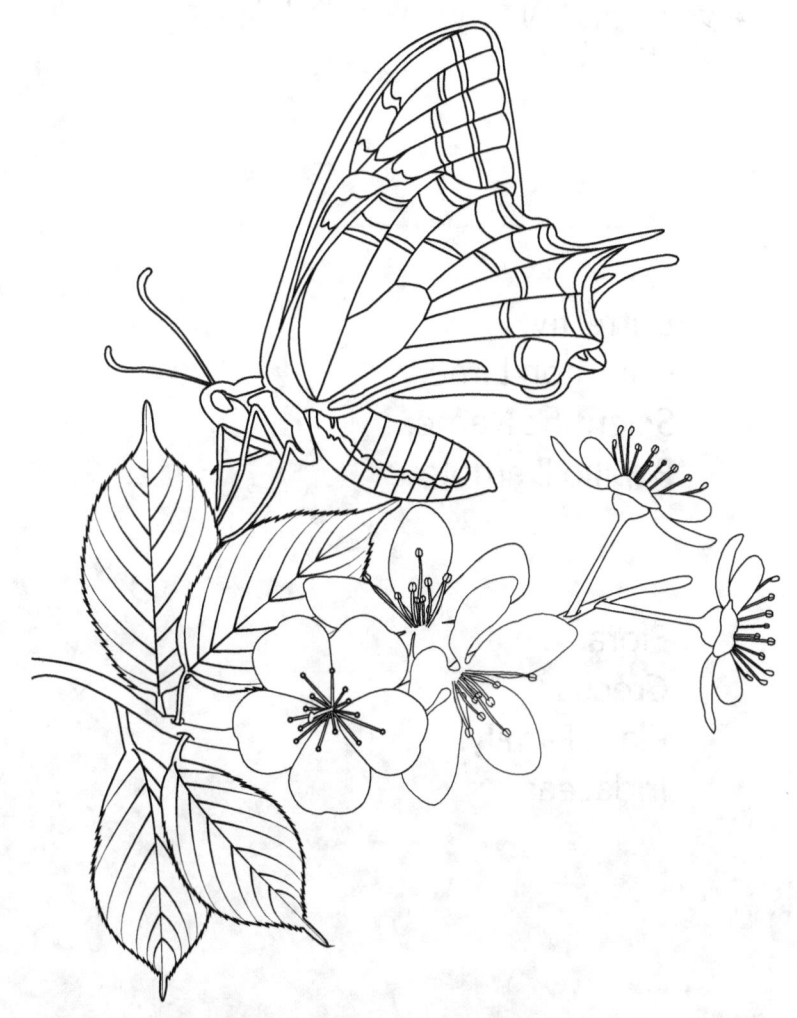

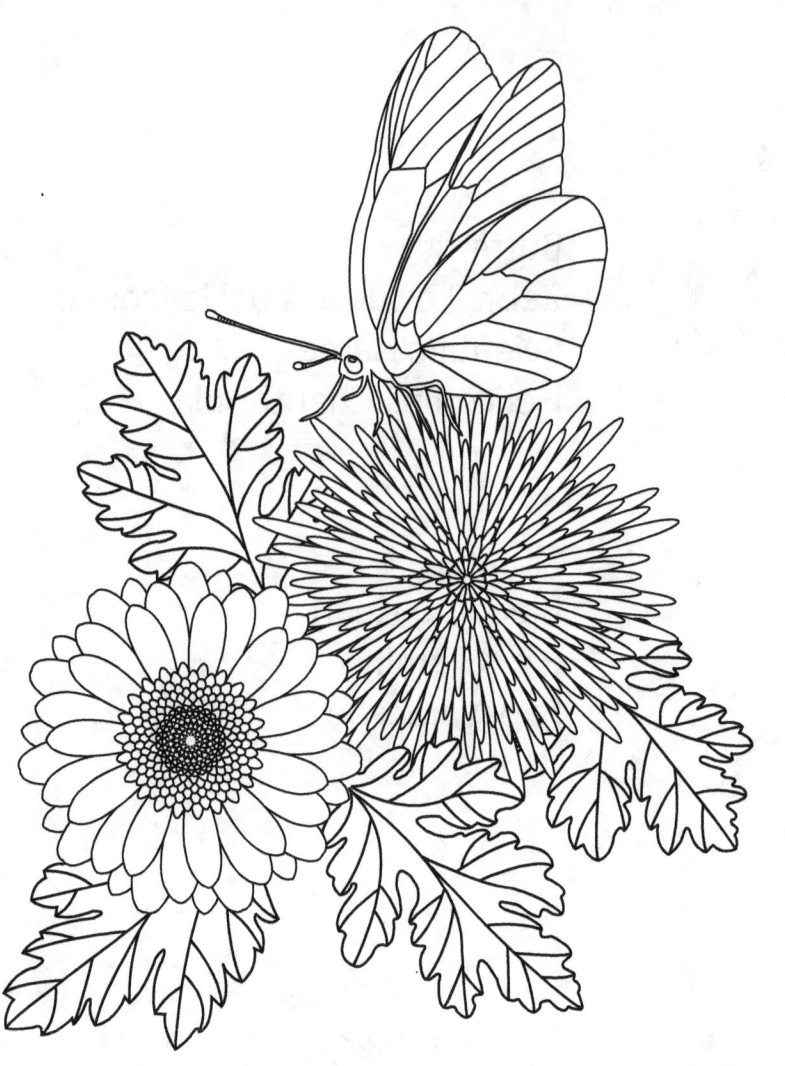

Butterfly:
Black Veined White
Scientific Name:
Aporia Crataegi

Flora:
Chrysanthemums
Plant Family:
Asteraceae

Butterfly:
Common Lime
Scientific Name:
Papilio Demoleus

Flora:
Crocus
Plant Family:
Iridaceae

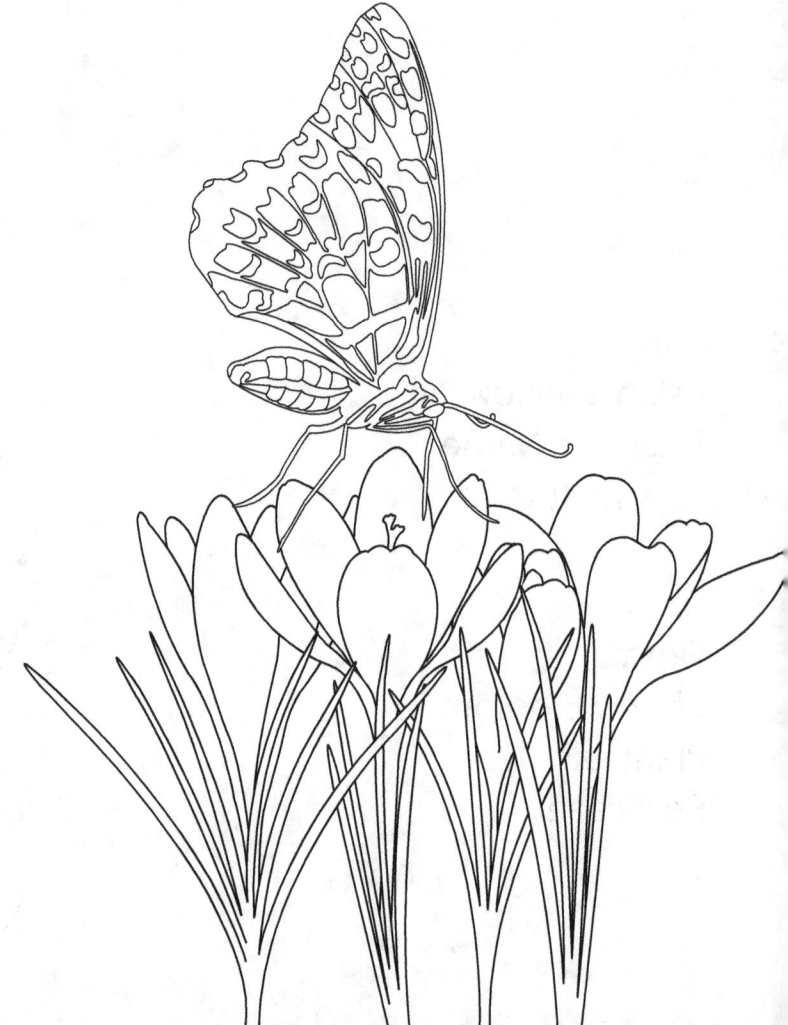

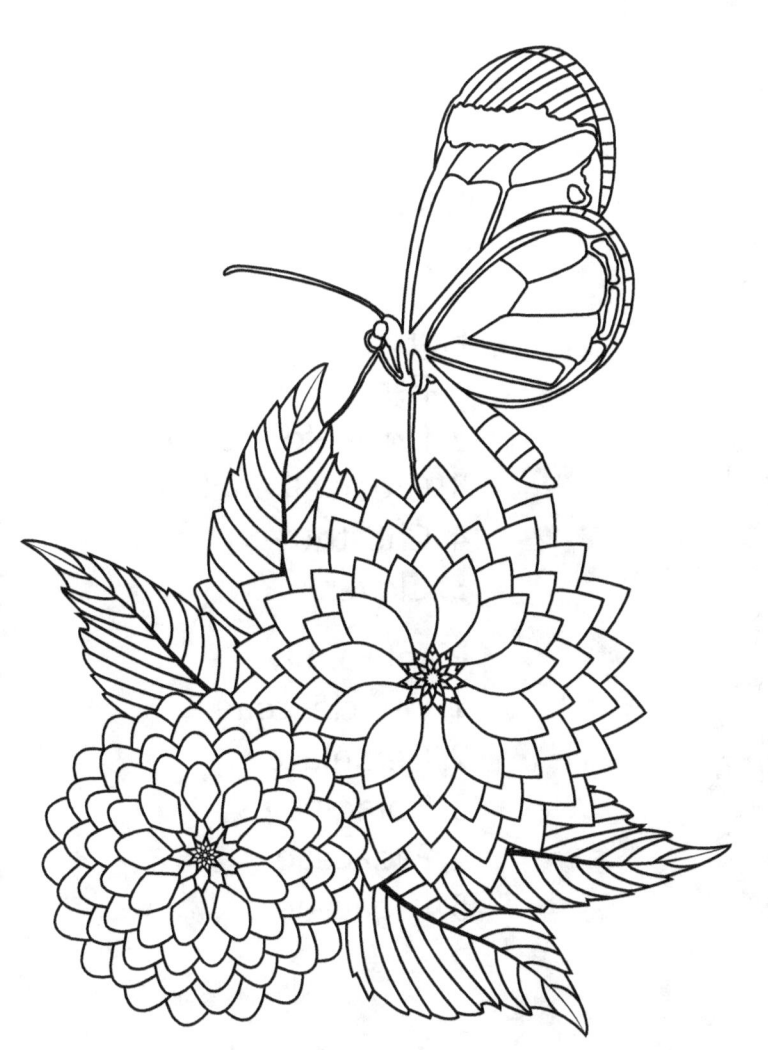

Butterfly:
Glasswing
Scientific Name:
Greta Oto

Flora:
Dahlias
Plant Family:
Asteraceae

Butterfly:
Green Veined White
Scientific Name:
Pieris Napi

Flora:
Fuchsia
Plant Family:
Onagraceae

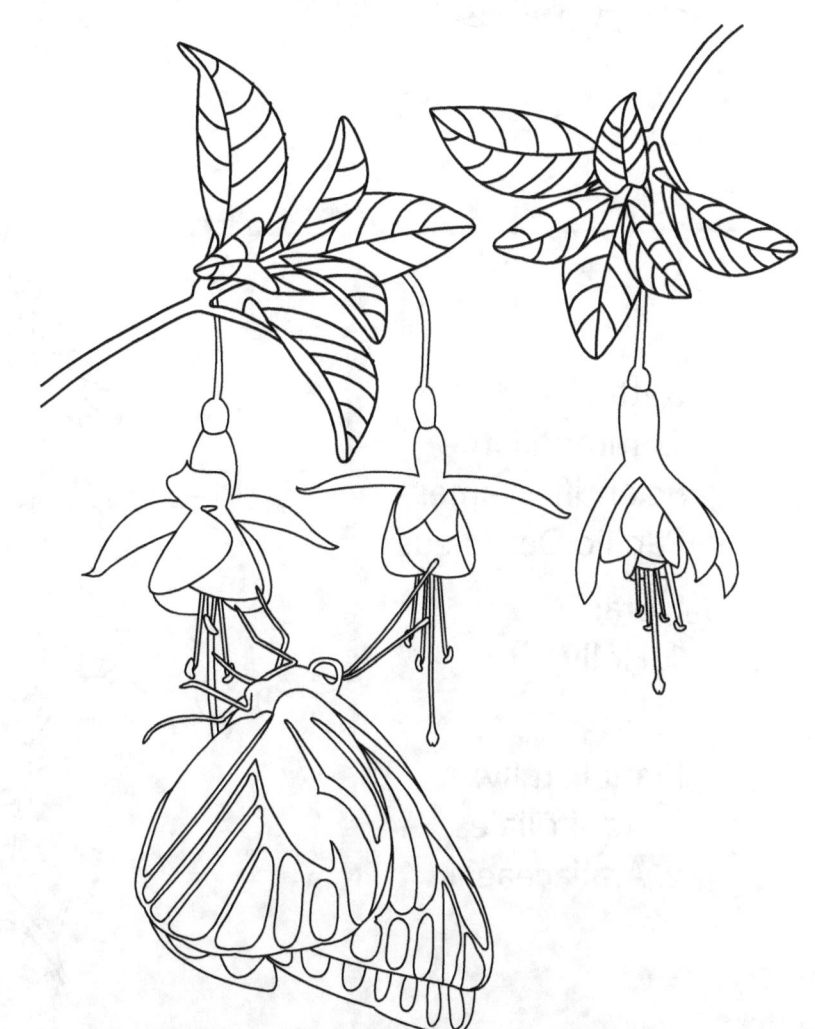

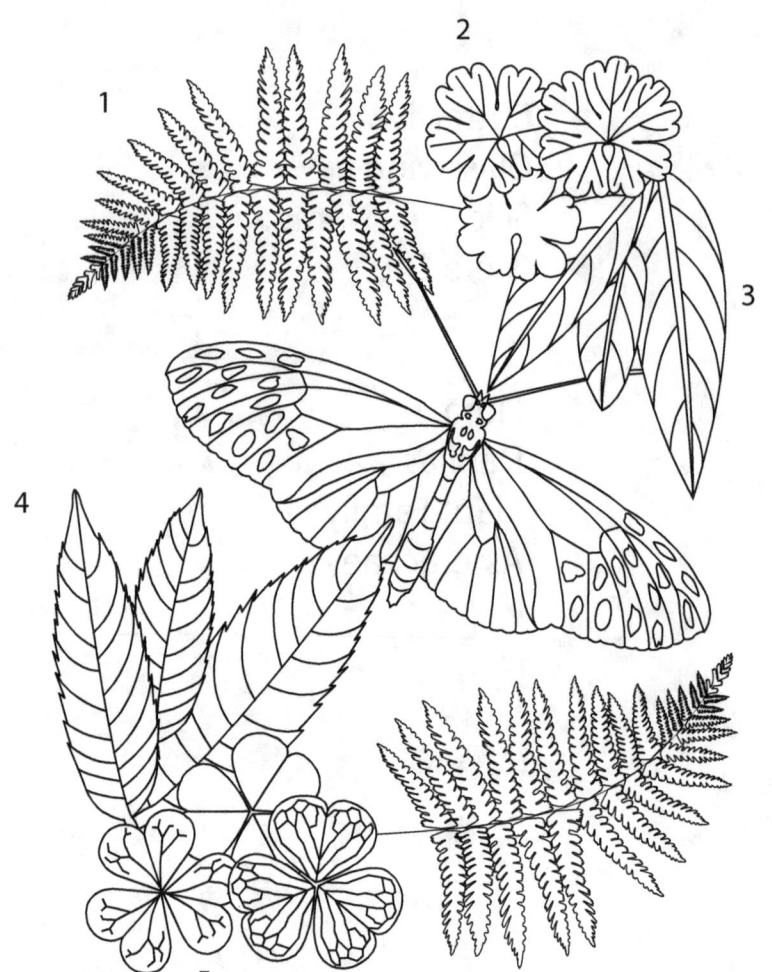

Butterfly:
Doris Longwing
Scientific Name:
Laparus Doris

Flora:
1. Fern
2. Doves-foot cranesbill
3. Green alkanet
4. Chestnut
5. Clover

Plant Family:
1. Onocleaceae
2. Geraniaceae
3. Boraginales
4. Fagaceae
5. Fagaceae

Butterfly:
Common Lime
Scientific Name:
Papilio Demoleus

Flora:
1. Holly
2. Ivy

Plant Family:
1. Aquifoliales
2. Araliaceae

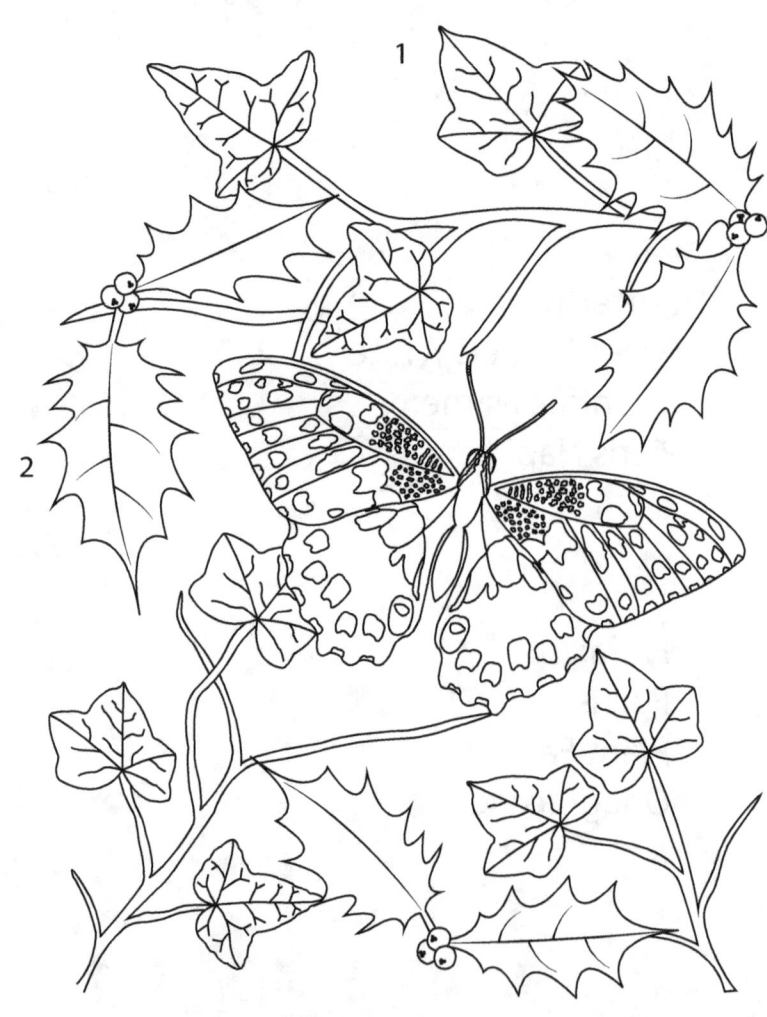

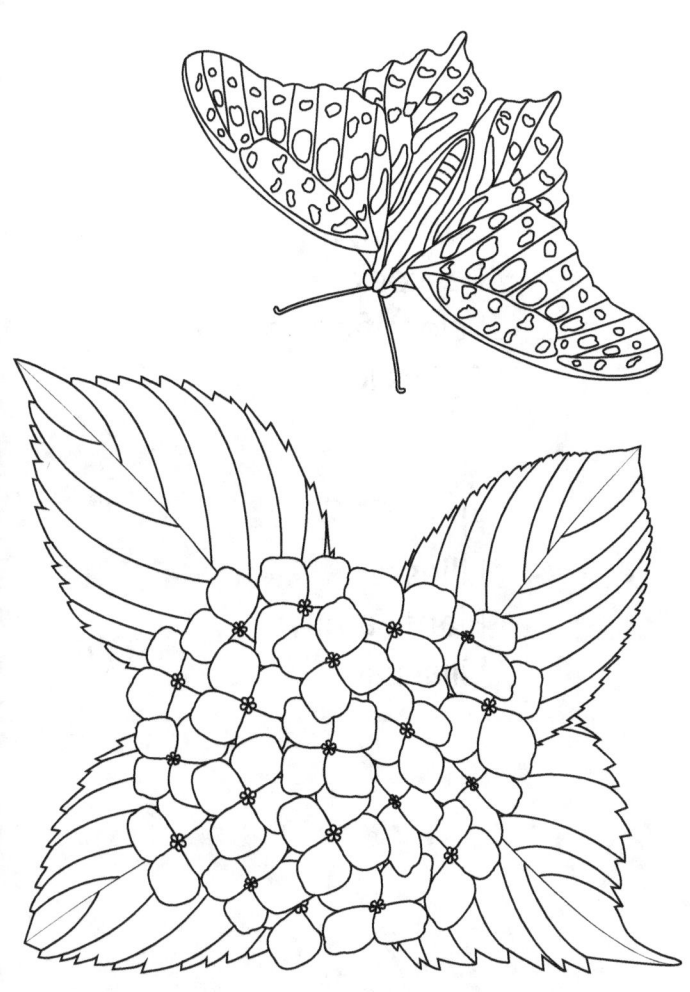

Butterfly:
Malachite
Scientific Name:
Siproeta Stelenes

Flora:
Hydrangea
Plant Family:
Hydrangeaceae

Butterfly:
Eastern Tiger Swallowtail
Scientific Name:
Papilio Glaucus

Flora:
1. Aralia
2. Beech
3. Ash
4. Sycamore
5. Rowan
6. Wild Service

Plant Family:
1. Araliaceae
2. Fagaceae
3. Oleaceae
4. Sapindaceae
5. Rosaceae
6. Rosaceae

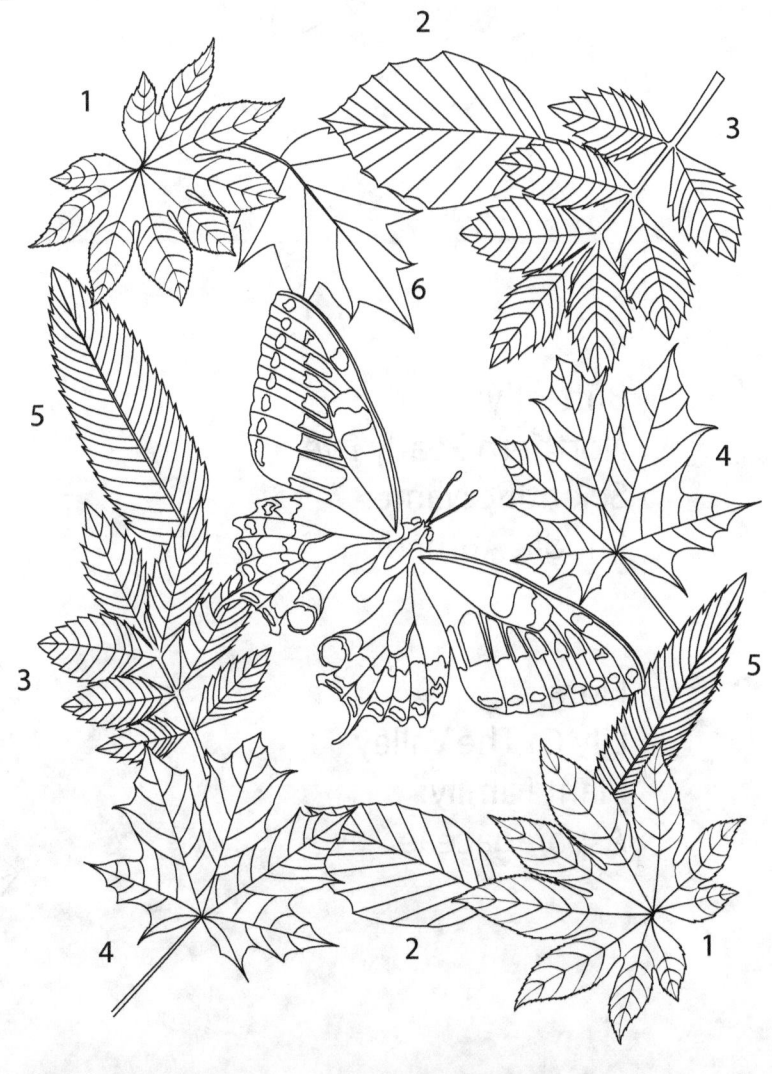

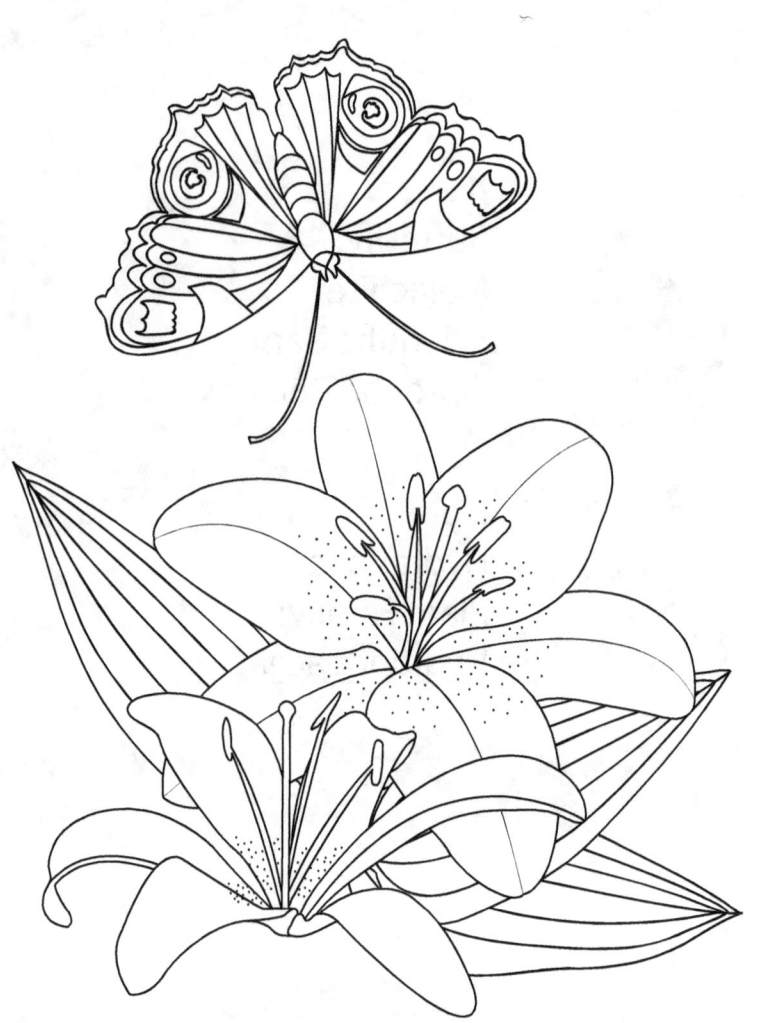

Butterfly:
Peacock
Scientific Name:
Aglais Io

Flora:
Lilies
Plant Family:
Liliaceae

Butterfly:
Northern Pearly Eye
Scientific Name:
Enodia Anthedon

Flora:
Lily Of The Valley
Plant Family:
Asparagaceae

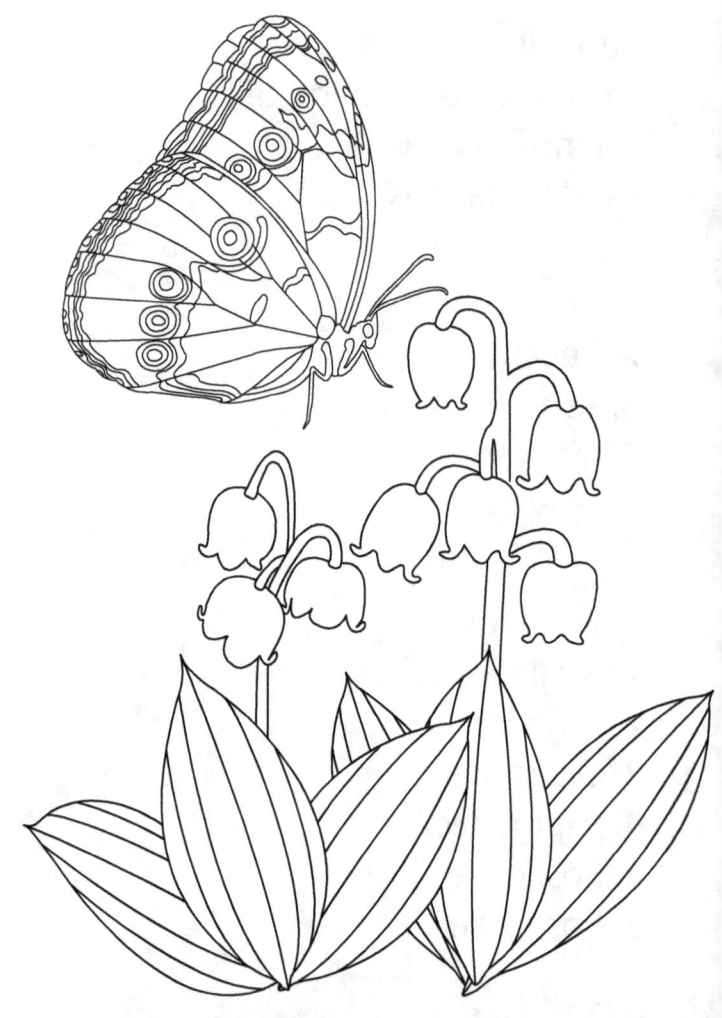

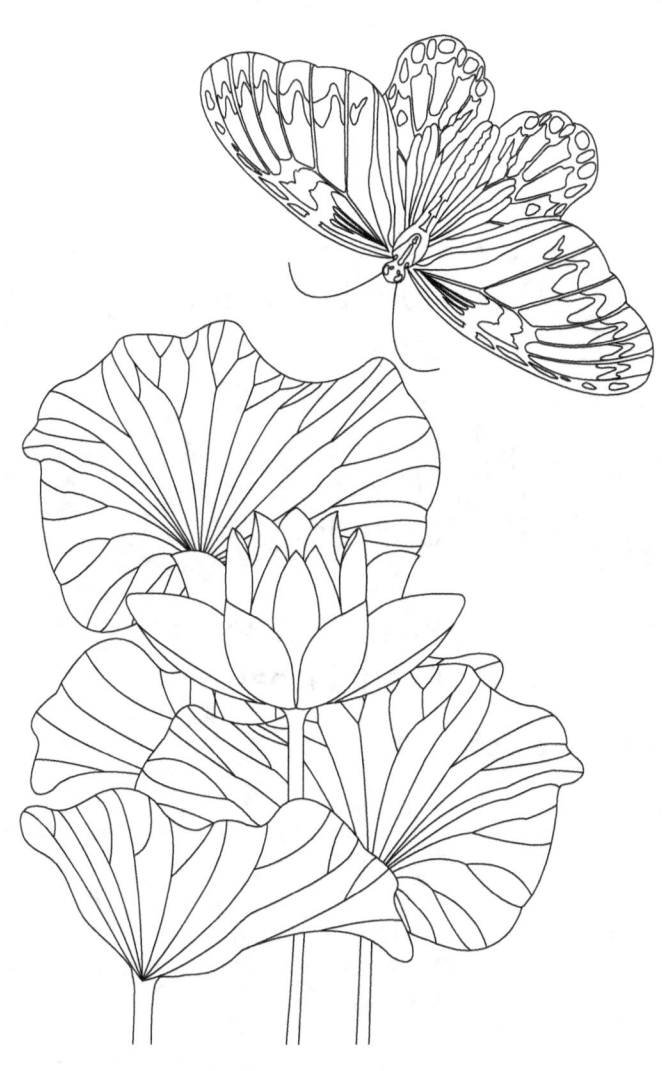

Butterfly:
Marbled White
Scientific Name:
Melanargia

Flora:
Lotus

Plant Family:
Nymphaceaea

Butterfly:
Morpho
Scientific Name:
Morpho Peleides

Flora:
1. Oak Leaves
2. Acorns

Plant Family:
1. Fagaceae
2. Fagaceae

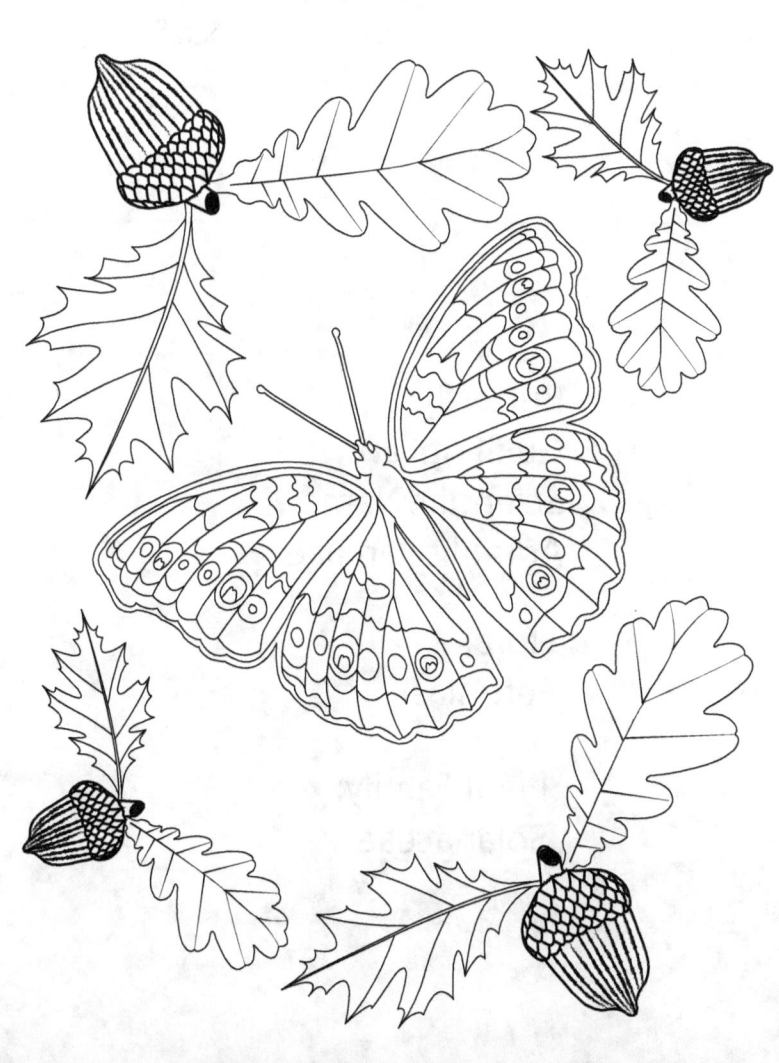

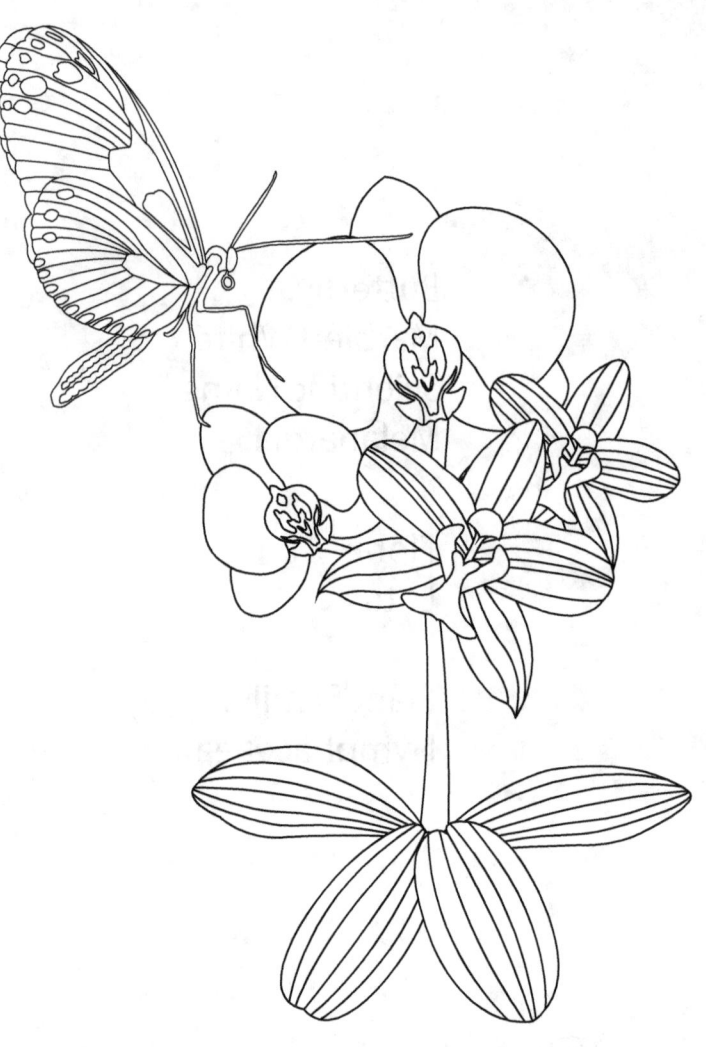

Butterfly:
Doris Longwing
Scientific Name:
Laparus Doris

Flora:
Orchids

Plant Family:
Orchidaceae

Butterfly:
Gulf Fritillary
Scientific Name:
Agraulis Vanillae

Flora:
Petunias

Plant Family:
Solanaceae

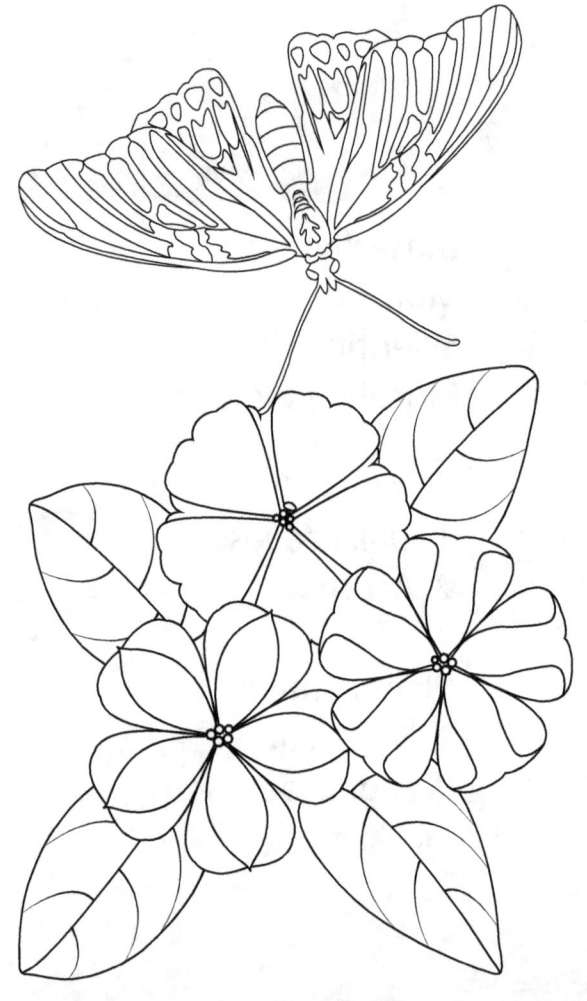

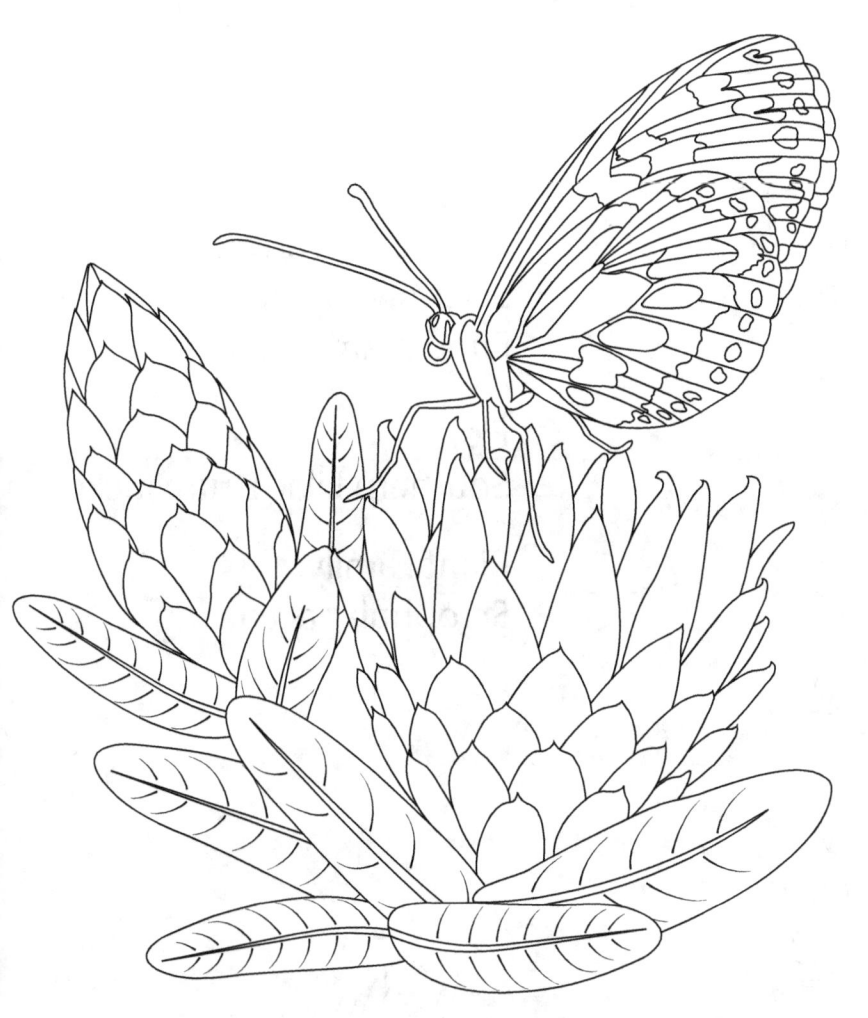

Butterfly:
Tiger Longwing
Scientific Name:
Heliconius Hecale

Flora:
Proteas

Plant Family:
Proteaceae

Butterfly:
Common Mormon
Scientific Name:
Papilio Polytes

Flora:
Roses

Plant Family:
Rosaceae

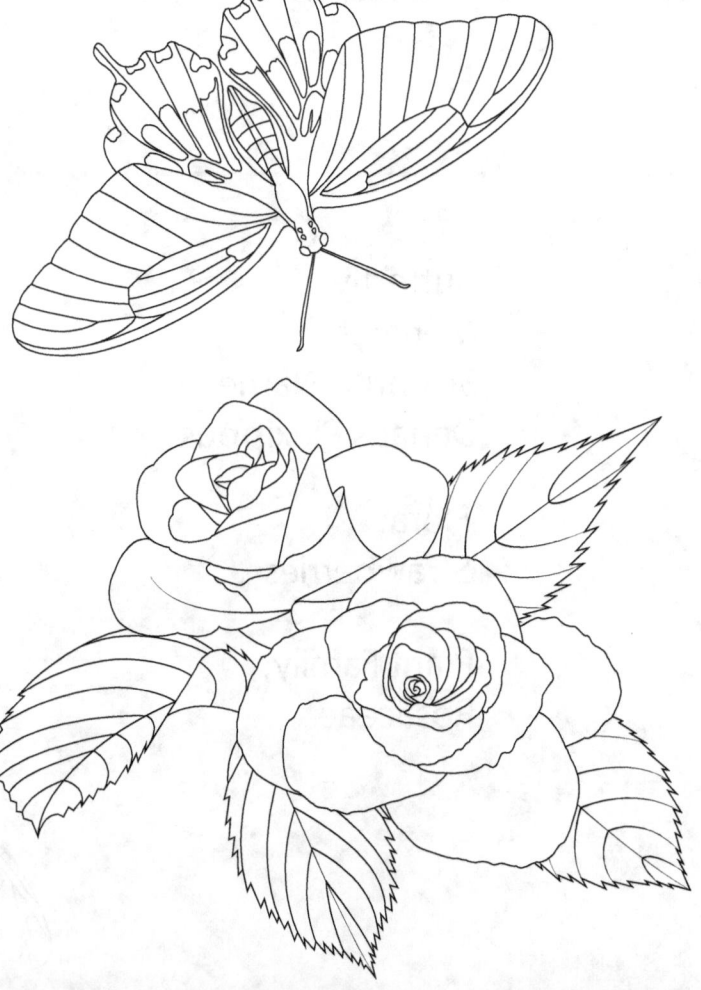

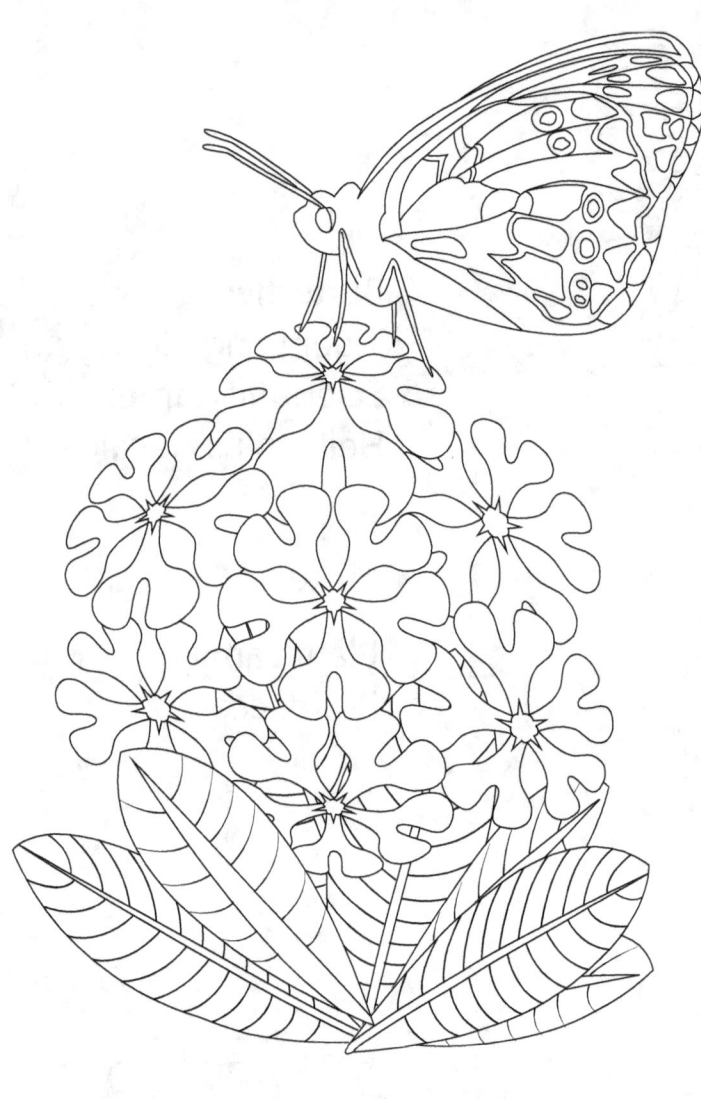

Butterfly:
Northern Pearly Eye
Scientific Name:
Enodia Anthedon

Flora:
Southern Lilac Drumsticks

Plant Family:
Scrophulariaceae

Butterfly:
Monarch
Scientific Name:
Danaus Plexippus

Flora:
Strawberries

Plant Family:
Rosaceae

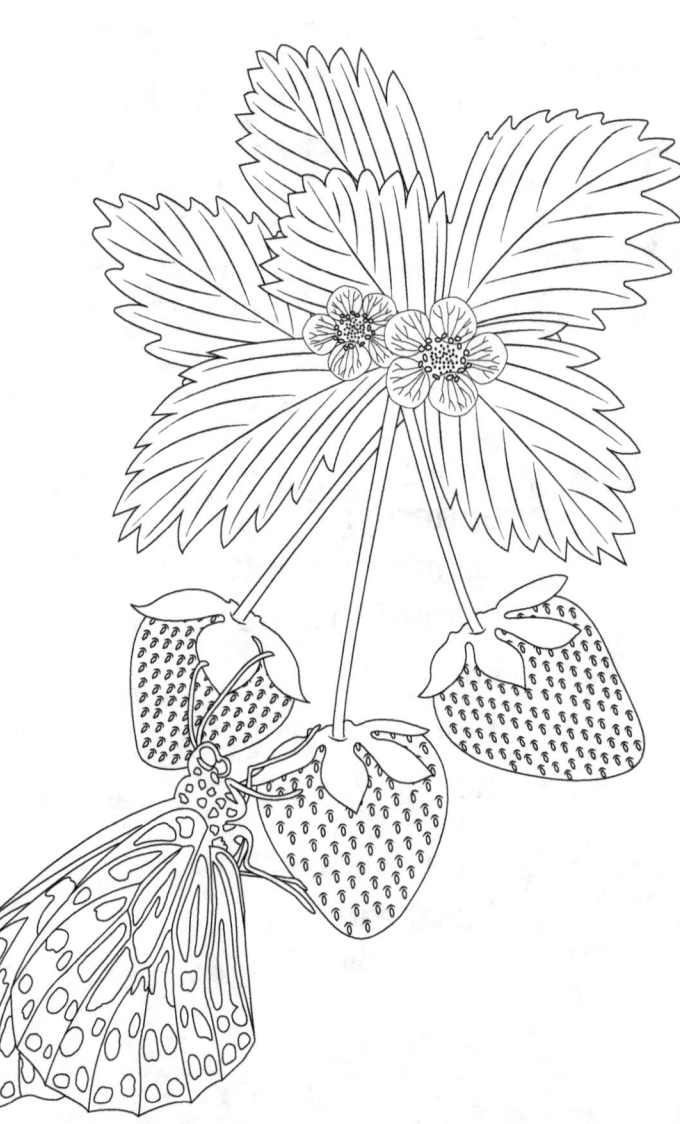

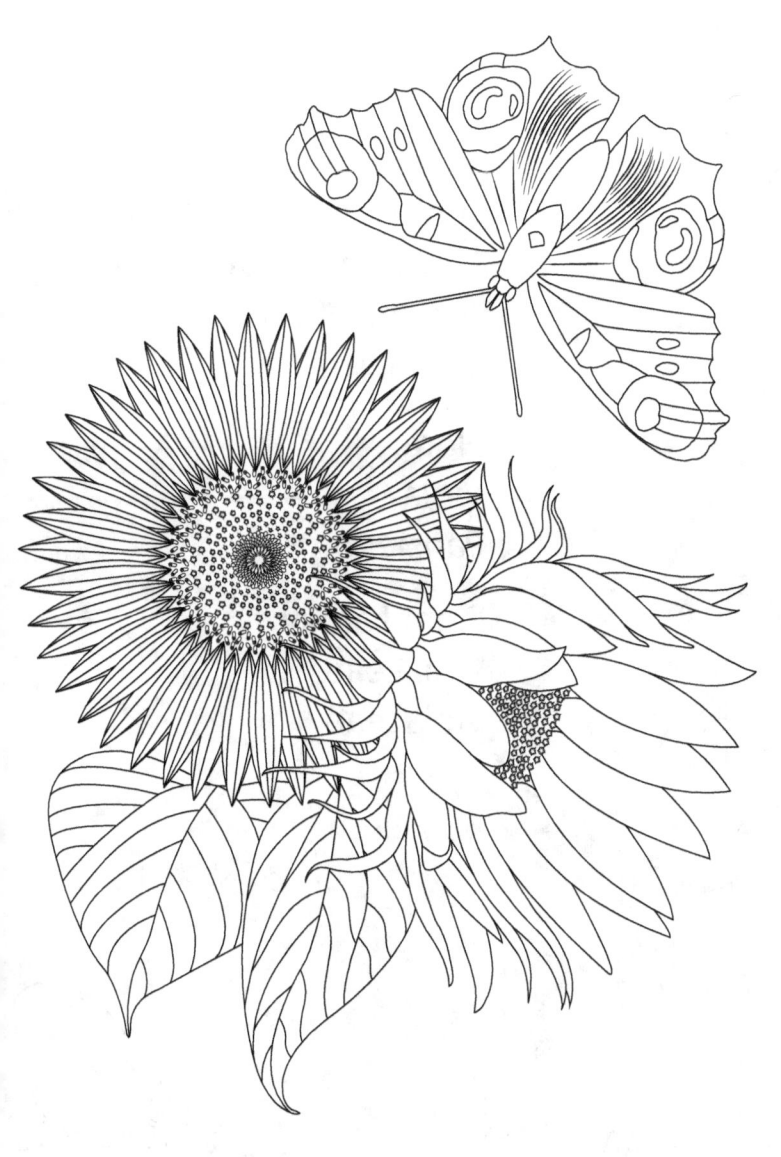

Butterfly:
European Peacock
Scientific Name:
Aglais Io

Flora:
Sunflowers

Plant Family:
Asteraceae

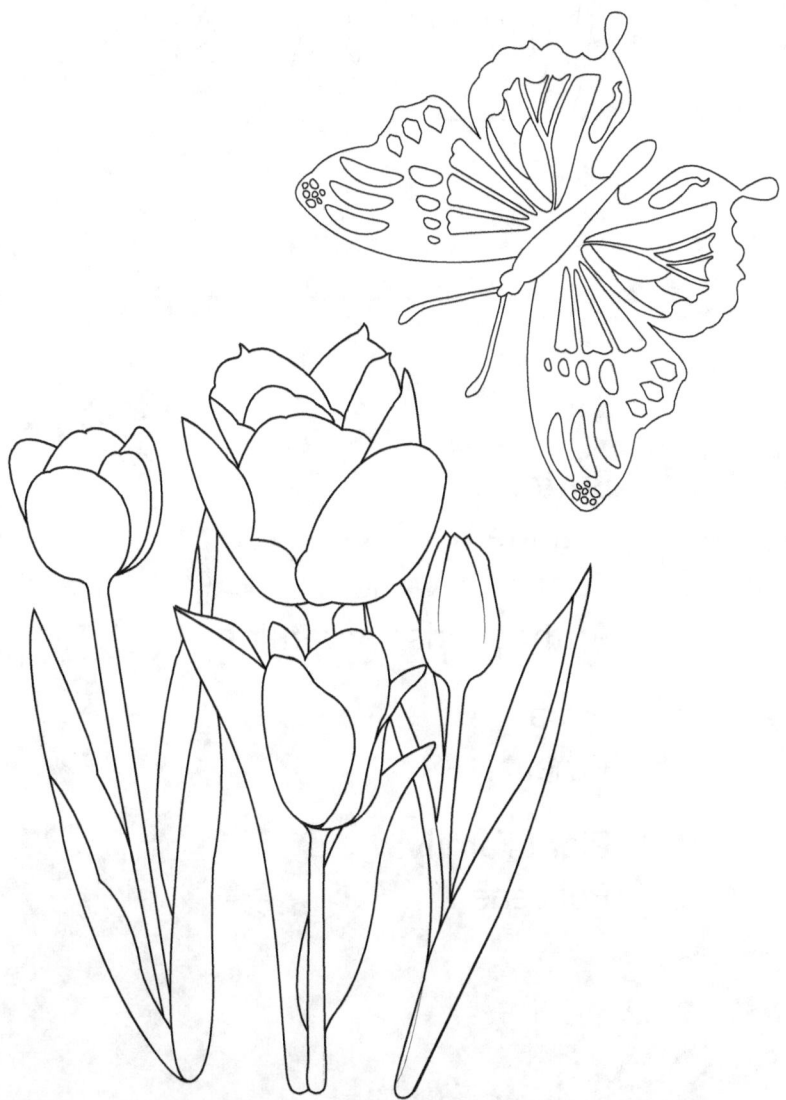

Butterfly:
Giant Swallowtail
Scientific Name:
Papilio Cresphontes

Flora:
Tulips

Plant Family:
Liliaceae

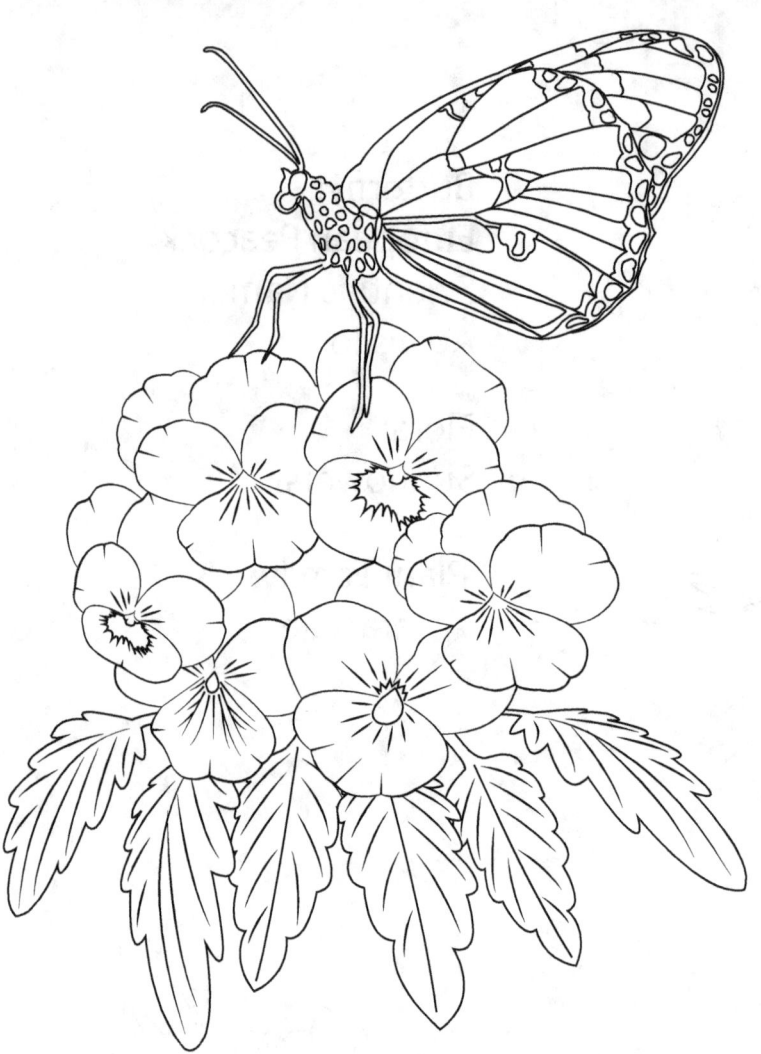

Butterfly:
African Admiral
Scientific Name:
Antanartia

Flora:
Viola
Pansies

Plant Family:
Violaceae
Violaceae

Butterfly:
Orange Tip
Scientific Name:
Anthocharis Cardamines

Flora:
Wheat

Plant Family:
Poaceae

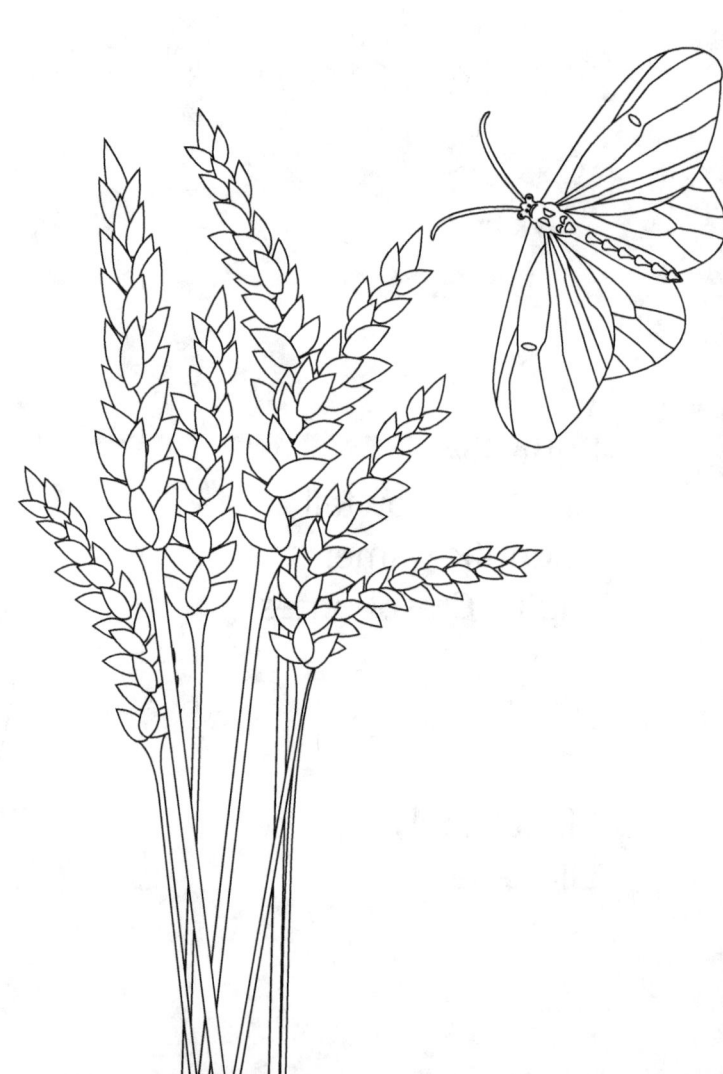

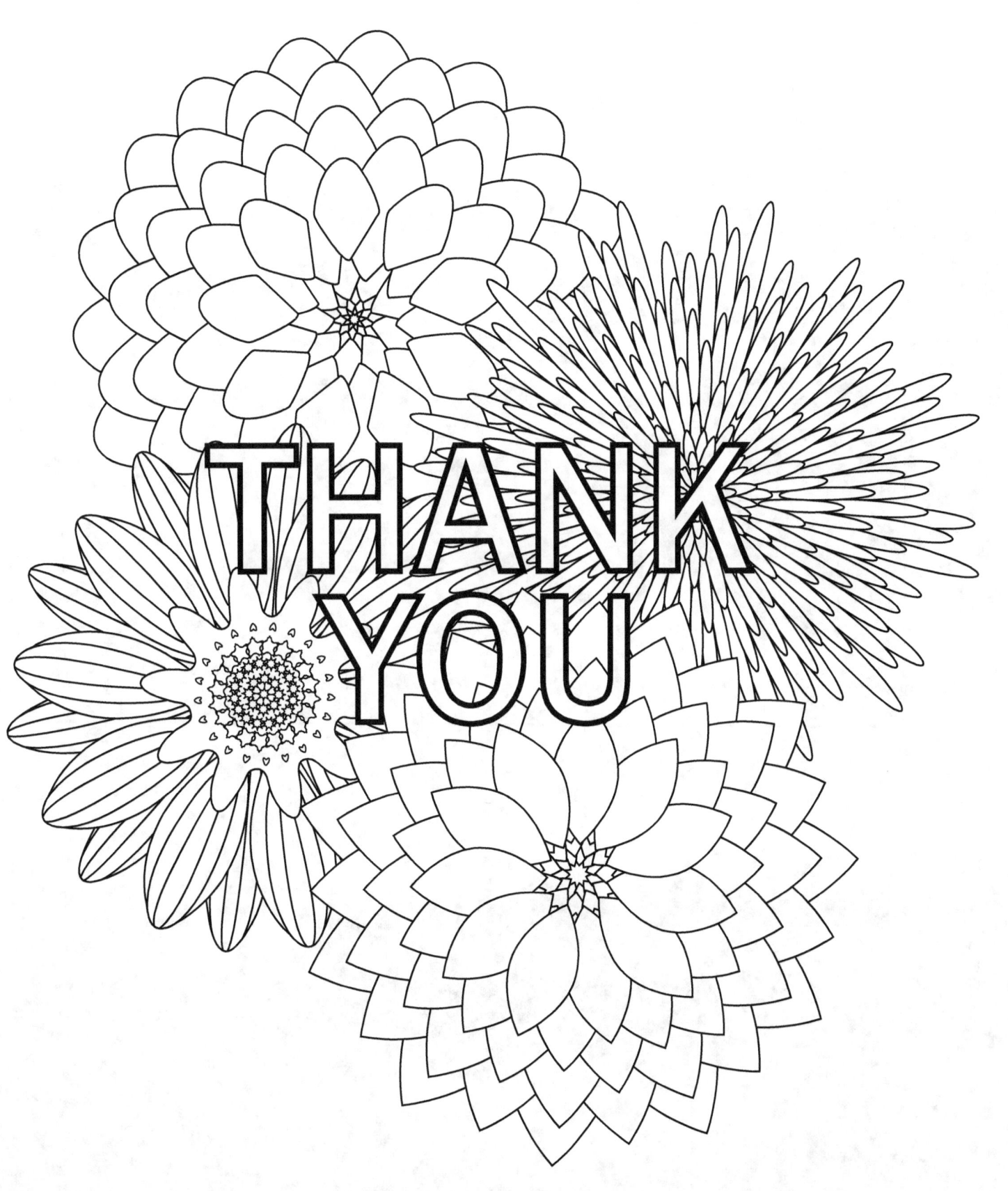